MARK CHILD

Discovering Churchyards

SHIRE PUBLICATIONS LTD

Contents

The cover photograph of Penn churchyard, Buckinghamshire, and the other photographs are by Cadbury Lamb.

To Lorraine Claire

Copyright © 1982 by Mark Child. First published 1982, reprinted 1989. Number 268 in the Discovering series. ISBN 0 85263 603 2.

Set in 9 on 9 point English Times by Permanent Typesetting & Printing Co Ltd, Hong Kong, and printed in Great Britain by C.I. Thomas & Sons (Haverfordwest) Ltd, Press Buildings, Merlins Bridge, Haverfordwest.

1. Introduction

Setting

The churchyard provides the eye with a setting for the church. If the building itself has a plain exterior it can only be enhanced by the way in which the grounds are kept. One's first impression is largely influenced by this, the location and setting. If sedge and nettles almost reach across the pathways, if at all times the tops of headstones just appear above a sea of grass, if the whole exudes an aura of disinterest and decay instead of even controlled untidiness – one instinctively feels that the same will be true of the church. The churchyard which is a mess may immediately tell us something about the state of the parish: that it is small – too small to keep up its church adequately – poor, uncaring or even non-existent.

Many churchyards are overgrown and untended. Some are cleared perhaps twice each year by a kind local with time on his hands; others are kept generally tidy. An increasing number are mown to a lawn, their tombstones uprooted and replanted elsewhere in sentinel order as perimeter fencing. The labour required to run a motor mower across a lawn once the ground has been levelled is far less than that required to scythe and shear between the headstones. Headstones may even be lying flat under the turf out of sight. In those churchyards which have so far escaped, a neatly clipped oasis indicates that the representative of some long established local family lives on. Almost everywhere controversy rages. Ecologists see the churchyard as one of the few places where natural life can develop as it should, and certainly the study of fauna and flora in country churchyards is very rewarding. Others would like to see their contents recorded and photographed, and the ground levelled.

The true reason for the state of the churchyard is not one which concerns the visitor; we simply form an opinion which influences our whole field of vision, extending to the church exterior which usually dominates the scene. In this respect one thinks immediately of Cornish churchyards. They have two great advantages: there is the temperate climate which allows a great variety of subtropical plants and other shrubs, which would elsewhere be considered exotic, to be easily grown in the west; and there is the intractable granite, which, since it neither readily takes to carving nor does it erode, provides a perfect and plain contrast to the surrounding foliage. **St Just-in-Roseland** is full of flowering shrubs and trees; **Mylor, St Erth** and **Gulval** are much the same. All along the coastal areas of Cornwall in particular it is hard to discern many of the green-grey and brownish granite buildings, nestling amidst dense foliage in steeply banked hollows. Elsewhere too there are beautiful and unspoilt churchyards.

Others are pretty, such as **Broughton-in-Furness**, Cumbria, in daffodil time. There are many examples in the Cotswolds. Visitors to the beautiful church at **Cirencester**, Gloucestershire, situated at the busiest part of this country town, might be forgiven for thinking there was no churchyard at all. Yet, hidden from the roadway at the east end, from where one may have an interesting view of the church, is a comfortable burial ground which has been used for centuries. Here is a typical example of an oasis of peace and quiet, surrounded by the bustle of town life, yet seemingly in the middle of the countryside. Other churchyards with fine settings include:

Ashton-under-Hill, Worcestershire; Astbury, Cheshire; Aylesbury, Buckinghamshire; Blanchland, Northumberland; Bottesford, Leicestershire; Branscombe, Devon; Brockham, Surrey; Cardington, Bedfordshire; Cavendish, Suffolk; Chiddingfold, Surrey; Dedham, Essex; East Dereham, Norfolk; Exton, Leicestershire; Fingest, Buckinghamshire; Fritton, Norfolk; Great Salkeld, Cumbria; Hawkshead, Cumbria; Hopesay, Shropshire; Keswick, Cumbria; Kirkoswald, Cumbria; Leigh, Surrey; Lenham, Kent; Lower Peover, Cheshire; Nether Winchendon, Buckinghamshire; New Buckenham, Norfolk; Oadby, Leicestershire; Oare, Somerset; Rydal, Cumbria; Snowshill, Gloucestershire; Taynton, Gloucestershire.

There are some places, too, where the church provides a setting for the churchyard; where it so dominates the skyline that it acts as a backdrop in the distance. This may be by reason of the church's dominant position, in juxaposition to other buildings as at **Aldbourne**, Wiltshire, and **Kersey**, Suffolk, or as at **Avebury**, Wiltshire, where a deep and wide churchyard separates it from the road. The large Suffolk 'wool' churches are fine examples: **Lavenham, Long Melford** and **Blythburgh** – the last benefiting from the fishing trade. There is so much of **Long Melford** and it is so intricately decorated that it can neither be viewed nor assimilated at once; the eye naturally drops for relief to the vast expanse of churchyard in the foreground. The same is largely true of the other two, which have more open grounds, the green in each case broken up by long pathways. **Lavenham** has a rural 'feel' of near perfection, its pathway being lined – and its whole churchyard punctuated – by neatly clipped round bushes; and the church beyond it is one of the most beautiful buildings in England.

There are many churchyards which provide a vantage point for fine views of the surrounding countryside. If tall modern buildings have not been built too close by, churches which were built on high points of strategic importance to prehistoric man (see 'Origins', in chapter 2) may still afford the best views in the area. **Wroughton**, Wiltshire, a lovingly looked-after churchyard, is a good example. Built on a hill now almost overlooking the ugly and piecemeal sprawl of nearby Swindon, it commands excellent views of the countryside to the north and north-west and of its industrial neighbour to the north-east. It is always worth looking outwards from a country churchyard and trying to get some idea of what the view might have been like when the church, or its predecessor, was built on the spot. In most cases it will give a better understanding of why the site was chosen, and often one will be able, apparently, to line it up with some other ancient or important site on the skyline (see 'Leys and dowsing' in chapter 2). Understanding what is around and beneath us in a churchyard is not simply a matter of digesting what is in close proximity or even in the immediate vicinity, but – if the churchyard is ancient – it must be looked at in relation to the surrounding countryside. In erecting his buildings and selecting his sites ancient man thought in a way which is unknown to us and his reasons continue to baffle archaeologists. In trying to visualise what he might have seen, we may gain some understanding of his actions. But as we are not able to feel the internal and external forces and factors which prompted him to venerate certain areas and make them of religious importance, we will perhaps never unravel many of his mysteries. There are fine views to be seen from churchyards all over the country, including:

Alston, Cumbria; Arley, Worcestershire; Bobbing, Kent; Brampton Ash, Northamptonshire; Bromfield, Cumbria; Delamere, Cheshire; Eaton, Leicestershire; Frindsbury, Kent; Grasmere, Cumbria; Hammerwich, Staffordshire; Herstmonceux, East Sussex; Kenley, Shropshire; Kirkby Lonsdale, Cumbria; North Kilworth, Leicestershire; Patrington, North Humberside; Penn, Buckinghamshire; Prees, Shropshire; Tanworth-in-Arden, Warwickshire; Thornton, Leicestershire; Willingale, Essex; Woodhead, Derbyshire.

The most pleasing settings are those which merge with their surroundings and do not jar the senses. There are those in which the church, churchyard memorials, buildings and walls are in the same or similar materials, such as **Bibury**, Gloucestershire. The most harmonious are those which are all built in local stone. They will have long since closed their churchyards for burials except, perhaps, for interments following cremation. The stone will by now have mellowed and eroded to the extent that the cursory glance cannot detect work spanning perhaps hundreds of years in the individual features.

Churchyards not long closed or still in active service will almost certainly have been invaded by foreign marbles, and here and there one may come across twentieth-century breaks with traditional designs marking individual graves. Concrete cubes, 'marble' circles and rough chunks of stone in no particular shape, mostly inlaid by small brasses, can be found. They are rarely of any size and many remain half hidden by grass even when the ground has recently been mown.

People tend to forget, in their insistence that they or their loved ones be individually commemorated, that there is no good historical reason for so doing. In the span of time the precedent has only relatively recently been set. It was first in the minds of the rich simply because they could afford such things and might anyway have been in some way benefactors of the church. The Victorians took monumental masonry out of the hands of the local craftsman, standardised designs and displayed them in catalogues for universal public consumption.

The headstone was available to all, and it is comforting to feel that in marking the spot of interment with a tangible reminder of the deceased the memory may linger longer. And, psychological-ly, it may be equally comforting to some to know that they will have an established plot in this life as a hedge against any uncer-tainty they may feel about life after death. This is the theme which constantly crops up in churchyard art: the tradesman who is depicted with his tools as if he may require them on the other side, or even the written virtues of benefactors which accompany them as some kind of reference. A fine example of a tradesman's headstone, showing the tools of his trade, is at **Lewes**, East Sussex, dated 1747.

Individually commemorated burials have both advantages and disadvantages. They give us the opportunity to study the design and lettering of our predecessors, their fashions and art. But this is not why they came about, nor is it part of their purpose today. They tell us exactly where certain people are buried, but only if still *in situ*, and this is important to persons who may come from far away, seeking an actual site but having no directions beyond the boundary wall. Yet one only has to glance around any graveyard which is still in use to realise how quickly the good in-tentions fail in practice. There are the faded flowers on last week's burial, brown and mildewed, waiting to be transported to the rubbish heap and replaced. Other graves, not too old, are still being regularly tended whilst the condition of some indicates that they receive occasional attention at least, probably yearly. With exceptions, beyond that is the problem, and it increases with the size of the churchyard, especially in the small country parish.

Churchyards are cluttered with graves which have not been per-sonally tended for years; relatives have tired of the job, moved away from the area or themselves died – the last of the local line. Thousands of weather-stained, lichen-encrusted, eroded tomb-stones, which were once put up with the best of intentions, now tilt their legends at the sky. Memorials may not necessarily lean because they are on land which is exposed to high winds. (Some headstones in Cornwall are buttressed for this reason.) Trees are living and expanding things and their roots will eventually break up the soil around nearby monuments, causing subsidence. This will in turn tilt headstones and may place stresses on other monuments where there were never intended to be any, and as a result these may begin to collapse. Who will correct and repair? There are many churchyards in which modern headstones have been placed too close to trees, and equally as many which illustrate the foolishness of so doing in the past. A churchyard in this state will tell us as much about its parish as one which is overgrown. An unsightly array spoils the setting for the church, but what to do with the memorials which cause the problem may well be an expensive decision.

The problems of nature are less acute but — perhaps because of this — those of aesthetics are even more so in 'churchyard extensions'. These should not be confused with the municipal cemeteries, which are not discussed in this book, but are those pieces of land adjoining established churchyards which have been secured for further interments. The monuments are very likely to be mostly of the twentieth century, arranged in neat lines, composed of various 'marbles' with black lettering. Apart from the good order of things and overall uniformity, the most striking difference as one passes from an old churchyard into a new extension is likely to be the lack of foliage. The trees, bushes and shrubs which were so important to our ancestors, whether for effect, beliefs or use, seem to have little place in the neat arrangement of the extension. Individuals — and even this may be of pagan origin — may occasionally plant holly or laurel bushes on single plots. But this does nothing to enhance the setting of either the grounds themselves or the church, churchyard and extension as an integral unit.

Associations

'Tis now the very witching time of night,
When churchyards yawn, and hell itself breathes out
Contagion to this world.' William Shakespeare, *Hamlet*.

There are few places more certain to elicit an emotional response than a churchyard. It inspires the feeling that what may be a peaceful place, warm and light with the scent of grasses by day, is different after dark. Folklore often insists, and church guidebooks record and so help to keep alive the idea, that the sensitive person may well encounter a spectre of some sort. These range from ghostly black (or white) nuns to chariots and horses reputed to hurtle alongside the churchyard wall, as at **Stratton St Margaret**, Wiltshire. Popular belief is always full of commercial potential, although most people passing through a churchyard have at least half a mind on the purpose of the grounds. If they feel the sense of peace so beloved of guidebook descriptions where the grounds are considered to be 'well kept', it is an uneasy peace. Yet it is tinged with a strange assurance by the fact of those who lie around them. This feeling is exemplified by the 'Reader on me cast an eye/As you are now so once was I' type of epitaph, a common form to be met with almost everywhere.

The last words of Thomas Gainsborough are reported to have been: 'We are all going to heaven, and Van Dyck is of the company.' The fact of death the leveller is more apparent in the churchyard than in the church itself, where the tombs and monuments are mostly of well-to-do persons and families. Outside it is different, and whilst those who could afford it might have shown some sign of their affluence in their memorial, they are themselves sunk in the same ground and in a state similar to that of their neighbours who may be in more humbly marked or even unmarked plots.

The fact of death has always inspired writers, be they locals putting together a few words to accompany a friend into the hereafter or famous men of letters. Rudyard Kipling provided an inscription for the cenotaph to the war dead in the churchyard at **Shotley**, Suffolk. The poet Thomas Hardy in 'The Levelled Churchyard' considered a subject which is controversial today. But the best known literary association is Thomas Gray's 'Elegy Written in a Country Churchyard', reminiscences on a balmy evening at **Stoke Poges**, Buckinghamshire, and the poet Shelley composed the less known 'Stanzas in Lechlade Churchyard' at **Lechlade**, Gloucestershire.

Some churchyards which contain famous graves are:

Aylsham, Norfolk: Humphry Repton (landscape gardener).
Balquhidder, Perthshire: Rob Roy.
Bonchurch, Isle of Wight: Algernon Swinburne.
Bromham, Wiltshire: Thomas Moore.
Caldbeck, Cumbria: John Peel.
Coniston, Cumbria: John Ruskin.
Dorking, Surrey: George Meredith.
East Coker, Somerset: T. S. Eliot; William Dampier (sailor, explorer).
East Dereham, Norfolk: William Cowper.
East Stoke, Nottinghamshire: Lord Pauncefoot (Britain's first ambassador to the USA).
Ebchester, Durham: Robert Smith Surtees.
Eskdale, Cumbria: Thomas Dobson (sometime master of Eskdale hounds); depicts fox, hounds and hunting equipment.
Ewelme, Oxfordshire: Jerome K. Jerome.
Freshwater, Isle of Wight: Lady Tennyson.
Frimley, Surrey: Francis Bret Harte.
Grasmere, Cumbria: William Wordsworth.
Haughton-le-Skerne, Durham: William Bewick.
Haworth, West Yorkshire: the Brontes.
Horton, Staffordshire: George Heath (poet).

Itchen Abbas, Hampshire: John Hughes (said to be the last man to be hanged for horse stealing).

Keswick, Cumbria: Robert Southey; H. D. Rawnsley (co-founder of National Trust).

Kew, Greater London: Thomas Gainsborough.

Knutsford, Cheshire: Mrs Gaskell.

Leatherhead, Surrey: Anthony Hope.

Limpsfield, Surrey: Frederick Delius.

Little Marlow, Buckinghamshire: Edgar Wallace.

Lydford, Devon: George Routleigh (watchmaker, whose long memorial inscription includes many puns on his calling).

Lymington, Hampshire: Coventry Patmore.

Lyndhurst, Hampshire: Alice Hargreaves (nee Liddell: the 'Alice' in Wonderland).

Minstead, Hampshire: Arthur Conan Doyle.

Moreton, Dorset: T. E. Lawrence (of Arabia).

Newchapel, Staffordshire: James Brindley (engineer).

Petersfield, Hampshire: John Small (cricketer).

St Mary in the Marsh, Kent: E. Nesbitt.

Stamford, Lincolnshire: Daniel Lambert (the biggest Englishman).

Sutton Courtenay, Oxfordshire: George Orwell.

Swinbrook, Oxfordshire: Unity Mitford.

The celebrities in the churchyards and cemeteries of London are too numerous for even a selection to be listed here. Those who would pursue this subject can find a comprehensive list in *Harrap's Guide to Famous London Graves* by Conrad Bailey (Harrap, 1975).

Sometimes one may come across parts of the churchyard which include interesting burials other than those of known celebrities:

Bettws-y-Crwyn, Shropshire: late seventeenth-century grave of a pedlar, there laid to rest following a dispute between neighbouring parishes about which should bury him.

Brockenhurst, Hampshire: a man who killed adders in the New Forest.

Claverley, Shropshire: victims of the Black Death, 1349.

Eyam, Derbyshire: plague victims.

Happisburgh, Norfolk: sailors' graveyard.

Harrington, Northamptonshire: the dead of the battle of Naseby.

Hathersage, Derbyshire: mound reputed to cover Little John.

Hutton Rudby, North Yorkshire: grave of those who died in a cholera outbreak, 1832.

Ross-on-Wye, Herefordshire: plague victims, 1637.

St Mawgan, Cornwall: headboard commemorates ten men who froze to death in a boat, from the stern of which the headboard is reputedly made.

Thursley, Surrey: unknown sailor murdered at Hindhead, 1786.

Westham, East Sussex: plague victims, 1666, commemorated by four stones arranged as a cross.
Weston-on-Trent, Staffordshire: the dead of the battle of Hopton Heath.
Westonzoyland, Somerset: the dead of the battle of Sedgemoor.

2. History of the churchyard

Origins

A large number of churchyards are on land which was originally used for some kind of pagan ceremony. People remained heathen in their souls long after they had theoretically been converted to Christianity. As the old fears died hard, many churches were first built inside the protection of prehistoric enclosures. Where a former pagan site was purified and dedicated to Christianity, there would be established the ground area on which the churchyard was later to be added. Some churches are today encircled by ancient earthworks of approximately the same shape as the churchyard, which is then clearly much older than the associated church. The first burials on that spot, and therefore the religious ceremonies which took place there, are sure to have been pagan. When the Romans came they brought with them a preference for rectangular burial grounds, and this shape continued after the Norman Conquest. The Romans preferred cemeteries away from the place of worship, but this practice was not generally applied until overcrowding of churchyards by the mid nineteenth century made it a matter of necessity.

The churchyard may today be on or include a prehistoric burial mound, or such a mound may be found nearby outside the churchyard. A circular churchyard, such as **Wirksworth**, Derbyshire, **St Buryan**, Cornwall, or **Rudston**, Humberside, is likely to be very old, and those which are both circular and on mounds, such as **Edlesborough**, Buckinghamshire, and **Winwick**, Northamptonshire, may well have been used in prehistoric times. Such high points should not be confused with churches in very flat areas which are built on artificial mounds for the purpose of keeping them above the potential flood level. **Llandysilio**, Powys, has a modern church in an ancient churchyard; otherwise there are a great many round churchyards on mounds in Powys (formerly Breconshire, Montgomeryshire and Radnorshire) as well as in parts of south-west England. At **Berwick**, East Sussex, there is a Saxon barrow in the churchyard. **Maxey**, Cambridgeshire, is on a mound. Evidence that an area has had centuries of use has sometimes resulted from churchyard 'finds':

Roman pottery was discovered at **Kirby Bellars**, Leicestershire, and an Anglo-Saxon cup in gold and enamel at **Ormside**, Cumbria. At **Tilshead**, Wiltshire, were found more than forty skeletons, supposed to be those of invading Danes, interred without coffins in hollowed-out chalk. Much early churchyard art was predominantly pagan work adapted by cautious people for Christian use in a way that could be described as hedging their bets. The sacred and the profane were depicted together and the whole was usually executed in a manner which exemplified pagan feeling even when the motifs were Christian.

Christianity is thought to have reached Britain by way of Gaul in either the second or third century AD. At that time only the coastal areas seemed receptive and the supremacy of the Roman religion continued. A number of churches were later built on sites of Romano-British significance. For the next five centuries or so the success of the faith depended on the fortunes of the recently converted areas in their skirmishes with territorial invaders. If a Christian leader was defeated or killed in battle by a heathen, such as happened in 627 when Edwin died at the hand of Penda of Mercia, the defeated region turned once again to their pagan gods. The tentative foothold Christianity had was expressed both in the position of the early churches and burial grounds and in the churchyard art, particularly as applied to early crosses.

Many of the difficulties experienced by the missionaries of Christianity stemmed from the people's insistence on continuing to venerate standing stones, and churches built near them, such as **Stanton Drew**, Avon, and **Avebury**, Wiltshire, were probably an attempt at compromise on the part of the missionaries. Occasionally, as at **Pewsey**, Wiltshire, huge sarsens form part of the foundations, or they may be built into churchyard walls. Whatever the original intention of these henges and grouped or isolated standing stones, they had acquired a religious significance which eventually passed into folklore, and many common beliefs and superstitions about them lasted into the twentieth century. Often ancient standing stones, which were pressed into the service of Christianity, were inscribed with sun symbols. For example, the wheelhead symbol comprising a circle enclosing a cross (see chapter 4) continued to be worshipped both as a Christian motif and as part of a fertility ritual. A churchyard ceremony which most probably has pagan origins and may echo sun worship, with which this form of ritual was associated, is that of clipping the church. It was formerly a popular event but is now performed only at **Painswick**, Gloucestershire, and **Wirksworth**, Derbyshire. Children encircle the church, holding hands and dancing.

The whole of the village at **Avebury**, Wiltshire, is within a prehistoric enclosure and that of **Breedon on the Hill**, Leicestershire, has evolved around a hillfort, the church itself being where once there was a Saxon monastery. The churchyards at **Finch-**

ampstead, Berkshire, **Mawnan** and **Kilkhampton**, Cornwall, are also enclosed by earthworks and at other places — such as **Lilbourne**, Northamptonshire, **Brinsop**, Herefordshire, **Brinklow**, Warwickshire, **Melling**, Lancashire, **Burton Overy**, Leicestershire, and **West Wycombe**, Buckinghamshire — they are nearby. The (now ruined) church at **Knowlton**, Dorset, was built in the middle of a henge monument. The sites of **Brentor**, Devon, and **Coldred**, Kent, are enclosed by earthworks. **Ormside**, Cumbria, is on an artificial mound and **Crowhurst**, Surrey, at the top of a hill. When Pope Gregory I sent St Augustine to convert the heathens of Britain in 597 he specified that the pagan temples should be converted to the new religion. It was a shrewd idea in theory since it allowed for continuity of worship in the same place and people were less likely to resist for so long if they could retain the old venue for their devotions. Also, those who were not happy about the new religion, even after their leader and the majority had been converted, could do little about it once the place had been purified for Christianity. Besides, the practice underlined what the missionaries were saying about the omnipotence of the new God in that he was able not only entirely to supplant the gods of old, but to imbue their former place of worship with his presence.

Gregory's idea may not have been as universally put into practice as he had anticipated. Augustine had builders in his own company and they were doubtless eager to show what they could do. But missionaries from other sources, particularly from the north-west, were also encouraged to found churches where there were standing stones or venerated places of worship. Nearby evidence of prehistoric activity may signify an original intention to use the site but perhaps more cautiously than the missionaries had in mind. Otherwise it may indicate that the church has evolved away from its original site.

This occasionally comes to light in archaeological excavations when the remains of an early church — perhaps an apse or even a chancel — are found in the churchyard, some way from the present building. Local legend often suggests reasons why many churches are where we now find them. A number concern the devil, either as himself or in the guise of another form of supernatural intervention. He had an annoying habit of moving stones from one place to another until the overworked builders finally gave in and put up the church where he wanted them to. The most reasonable explanation for this kind of tale has its origins in the early struggle of the Christian missionaries over their converts' former pagan beliefs. If we see the missionaries as the builders — perhaps disinclined to use the old sites — and the spirit of paganism as the devil, we can imagine a conflict between the missionaries, who wanted to build in one place, and the converts, who favoured another. These stories are often linked with churches sited on high ground or mounds – **Alfriston**, East Sussex, and **Uphill**, Avon, are famous examples – and in view of the former pagan use of high ground it seems reasonable to suggest this as the possible origin of the folklore.

The earliest signs of the new faith were stone crosses which came to be beautifully carved and which were often put up at a place of former heathen worship. They were known as 'preaching' or 'teaching' crosses and by the eighth century were established landmarks. Whilst the original intention was to mark a place of communal gathering for the purpose of religious instruction and worship, it doubtless became the spot around which followers of the faith were buried by choice. In the early days the precedent might have been set by the saint who was their teacher and minister. In AD 752 the Pope granted St Cuthbert permission to establish churchyards around churches. This formed the graveyard concept and the idea flourished among the holy men. The ground was consecrated by a bishop, its cardinal points being marked by wooden crosses. Even after individually marked graves came into vogue, wood was a favourite material for the memorial despite its impermanence.

To begin with, monks placed portable altars in front of the standing crosses. Eventually the communities built their own permanent altars and protected them from the elements by enclosing them in small cells. People lived in huts made of wattle and daub, a kind of basketwork of interwoven reeds held together and generally covered by a thick application of mud. It is likely that the cells which first protected the altars were also made in this way. The worshippers stayed outside until it occurred to them that they too could be protected from bad weather if they constructed a larger room adjoining the one which contained the altar. The idea of reserving an area for the altar had also come from within the single cell of the Irish oratory. To begin with it was placed at one end, and later in the adjacent chamber. Since Ireland was also the source of one of the great waves of Christian conversion, it is reasonable that the practice, common in that country, of burying their followers around the saints would be adopted elsewhere.

Awareness was a great factor used as an argument in early times to justify establishing graveyards around some tangible symbol of the faith, in preference to cemeteries on other sites. It was felt that those who passed the graves on their way to pray would be more inclined to do so for the souls of the departed if they had recently seen their last resting place, and also they would be encouraged to think about their own souls. A reminder of their own ultimate faith was not inappropriate at any time but was particularly useful while Christianity was still being established. If the graveyard included the grave of the saint or missionary at whose cross the preaching took place, so much the better.

Churches were built to the north of any central churchyard cross, so that the largest ground area was to the south. There the sun, when it shone, did so at its brightest. It was the realm of souls made good and consequently has the most (excluding modern extensions) and the oldest graves. The east, from whence the sun rises, was deemed to be the place of God's throne and therefore is the point towards which one worships before his altar. Man lives in the west, but evil spirits lurk in the north, where the rays of the sun do not linger. In medieval times devil's doors were provided in the north walls of churches and were left open during the service of baptism so that the child's evil spirits could leave in that direction. There, in the shadow of the church, were buried strangers, criminals, suicides, stillborn and unbaptised babies and later even highwaymen.

At first the area of the churchyard was undefined in extent. It was not enclosed and had no legal standing. The priests considered burial therein to be their prerogative. It was probably a mixture of the desire to be buried as closely as possible to their spiritual leaders in the community and good public relations on the part of the more enlightened priests in allowing it which led to the gradual acceptance of the laity into the same ground. People have always looked to their leaders and feel less apprehensive in times of doubt if they are of the company! Whether or not the physical extent of the first churchyards was adequate was hardly an important issue. The bishop made a roughly circular tour of consecration and that more or less set the boundary. Even before the Conquest people fled to their church in times of trouble and filled the churchyard with their animals and possessions when they were threatened. The consecrated area around the church was considered inviolate from the earliest times. Only the English Civil War was to prove the exception.

Medieval and later use

In Saxon times the churchyard was used as a place for taking oaths and dealing with disputes. What better place was there for men to establish secular matters of honour and expect them to be upheld than on consecrated ground? Justice was meted out around the churchyard cross, the tangible symbol not only of the faith but of the community obligation to it, and hence a focal point of community life.

To appreciate how use of the medieval churchyard developed in a way we would now consider improper, we must understand the way in which people thought five hundred to a thousand years ago. They were subject to pestilence, plague, hostility and impermanence. Their life expectancy was less than half our own. In the early days their minds were in turmoil, grappling with a need to substitute their fears by their hopes in the all-embracing God, and striving to reach him. In addition the parish was responsible for the upkeep of the nave and the priest had to look after the chancel. And so, in the course of time, matters of a secular nature became – for a while at least – inextricably mixed with the more religious. In a way it embodied the true meaning of community spirit.

In 1287 a Synod of Exeter decreed that secular pleas should not be heard in the churchyard. There is no evidence that this was effective although churchgoers sometimes themselves petitioned against excessive noise in the churchyard while services were taking place. The main culprit was a common market; vendors and pedlars spread their wares for sale on the tops of table tombs. Horses stood around in the churchyard and cock fighting took place on consecrated ground. Just as the medieval church was itself used for all kinds of religious and secular business people saw the churchyard much as we might now consider the village hall, open to almost any event depending only on its physical limitations. Naturally while the churchyard was held in freehold by the priest it was to his advantage to foster such feelings and activities from which he might supplement his income.

Bells were sometimes cast in the churchyard. With the perils of travel and the high cost of transport, it was more convenient to cast them on site. In this way bell founders established themselves in new areas. Prayers were said over the bells as they were made. Certain parts of the ceremonies associated with baptism, marriage and burial began and in some instances ended in the churchyard. People frequently passed through on their way to transact business in the church porch – which was also considered a right and proper place to make agreements of a binding nature – or in connection with the notices which were there displayed. As the church might variously have been used as an armoury or a wool store, depending on its location, the grounds would often have been visited by people concerned with these. Town churches in particular sometimes served as places of business for guildsmen or as libraries, and local children sometimes received schooling from the priest. Matters of tithes were resolved and inquests took place within their walls.

Itinerant merchants set up their stalls beside the church; strolling players and musicians performed and miracle plays took place. There were many children's churchyard games, of which fives is probably the best known survivor. At **Martock**, Somerset, one can still discern the holes which afforded footholds so that balls could be retrieved from the roof. Archers practised their skills and used the stone boundary walls and even the fabric of the church itself to sharpen their arrows. Although there were eventually local penalties for those who played sports in the churchyard, the grounds were used for football, single-stick playing and various contests until the nineteenth century.

Some churchyards were the scene of skirmishes during the Civil War and a number of churches exhibit cannonballs recovered from the fabric or environs. At **Alton**, Hampshire, the churchyard was the scene of a full battle, its defenders being forced back to die to a man within the church. Military prisoners were held at **Burford**, Oxfordshire, when Cromwell's men put down a Levellers' rising in 1649, and some of them were executed in the churchyard. The churches of **Cirencester, Painswick** and **Stow-on-the-Wold** in Gloucestershire were all used as prisons for Royalists during the Civil War. The state of churchyards so used must have been disgraceful, with soldiers trampling about them and tethering their horses in the grounds with scant regard for the nature of the place, as at **Beetham**, Cumbria. Prisoners taken at the battle of Sedgemoor in 1685 were locked in the church at **Westonzoyland**, Somerset.

The churchyard was busy at most times, but for the ordinary person the highlights were the fairs and feast days. The fair was the annual wake or revel of which the church was itself the main beneficiary. Proceeds helped to provide books, church plate, bell ropes and so on. Everyone was compelled to attend and the whole event achieved a huge following, probably helped by copious amounts of the local strong ale. This was brewed in the church house and sold at a price usually fixed by the local abbot. Dancing and games took place although people – theoretically at least – respected the south side of the grounds where the majority of the graves were and confined themselves to open spaces or the north side. The result was a riot of merrymaking, a colourful spectacle which mirrored the brightly painted interior of the church itself.

Animals were always a problem in the churchyard. The first graveyards were not enclosed and could easily be ravaged by cattle and other farm and domestic animals. It was considered important to protect the churchyard from destruction and desecration by livestock. There were frequent edicts by lords of the manor or parish overseers seeking to ensure that the owners of animals kept them out of the churchyard. Fines were levied against offenders. Slowly churchyards came to be enclosed, but while the people of the parish paid for the upkeep of the fencing to keep animals out of the churchyard, the priest sometimes raised money by letting out the grazing within. Indeed the idea of grazing animals in the churchyard persisted through Victorian times when they were often depicted in engravings, even to the present, when one may occasionally encounter sheep or goats.

The rector or vicar now holds the freehold of the churchyard, subject to the right of the deceased in the parish to be buried there. The parochial church council has to maintain it, but it is the duty of the churchwardens to see that it is only used for its proper purposes. Churchyards which are closed for burials still remain the responsibility of the parochial church council, although they may abdicate this to some other community body.

Leys and dowsing

It is not within the scope of this book to discuss in depth the question of so-called ley lines, although they must be mentioned as possibly having bearing on the siting of churches. This matter depends on what one believes or is prepared to accept, but those who plot leys find that there are many churchyards along their lengths. I use the word 'churchyards' and not 'churches', the most usual description for the point of contact, since, whilst the line of a ley will remain constant in the original theory at least church buildings may not still be standing on the site of their original foundation.

One simple definition of ley lines is that they were prehistoric straight tracks which include man-made sites or associated natural ones along their lengths, formerly as sighting aids for travellers. At least, this was the substance of Alfred Watkins's interpretation in 1921. The important landmarks tended to be the highest natural points, although not exclusively, or those on which earthworks or burial mounds were either made or in themselves created the high points. In their turn Christian churches were established at these spots of former pagan worship and hence now stand on or near a known ley. Where the church is no longer entirely on its original foundations, the ley may pass at some other point within the churchyard and on to the next feature — perhaps now also a church which can be seen in the distance.

It has been suggested that the axis of some churches was not aligned to the generally accepted east-west plane, but along the lines of a ley. And there is a further opinion that leys may not necessarily be straight tracks or once purely physical features on the landscape, but that they might be the lines of an energy-producing force known sensitively by our ancestors. Their shape and direction has in some instances been defined by dowsing. This is a method of searching for water, minerals and forces using divining rods or sticks, or similar apparatus, in combination with the diviner's own senses. Applied to the church and churchyard, it has been claimed that water lines apparently cross beneath the altars and tend to occur similarly beneath any ancient standing or otherwise religiously significant stones in the churchyard, even those which are thought to have been moved from elsewhere. When used to follow leys the method has suggested theories about their shape and intersection at points connected with ancient — and often modern — religious activity, although the church itself need not be, nor at any time have been in the past, the major point of contact. The ley may be felt to be centred upon some other object in the churchyard, such as a standing stone or an ancient burial mound.

It is interesting to speculate, as we stand in a churchyard which may be on high ground or have prehistoric remains nearby, on the original reason for putting it there. The church guidebook may tell you that the area has long been known to man and that the discovery of ancient burials in the vicinity attests to this and indicates its connections with pagan activity. Yet in many instances, if one is not to reject out of hand the theory of ley lines as elements of force, we must at least acknowledge that the force might have preceded the religion – to whichever gods! Just as pagan standing stones were altered in the cause of Christianity, so too were the old gods found names which were more appropriate as saints. The physical straight tracks may have evolved along the lines of the leys.

All of this is speculative and controversial and regarded by many as somewhat heretical. But it is something to be considered when visiting a churchyard – perhaps one at seemingly the end of a country lane. The matter should interest any visitor who wishes to be aware of his surroundings. I have seen churchyard dowsers at work divining for water, lost burials and metals with their rods and twigs, and others seeking activity of a different nature in the vicinity of churchyard tombs and mausoleums.

3. Into the grounds

Mounting steps

The approach to the churchyard may be past one, two or three ascending steps. These were used to help people mount their horses and are usually hewn out of a single block of stone and arranged so that they are at right angles to the roadway. Mounting steps were placed near the main entrance to the churchyard or otherwise close by the church porch. Where they are now in the latter position – and it is most unlikely that they will ever have been moved – in an enclosed churchyard, it is probable that the churchyard was not enclosed when they were put up. They are therefore more likely to be early examples of their type, and this is usually borne out by the extent to which each step has been worn to a deep, smooth curve, which in some cases may have all but eroded away the middle section of the risers. There are examples at **Bockleton**, Worcestershire, **Lowther** and **Kirkland**, Cumbria, **Altarnun** and **St Germoe**, Cornwall, **Fairfield**, Kent, **Chollerton**, Northumberland, and **Stokesay**, Shropshire. At **Ightham**, Kent, there are four steps by the gate.

Mounting steps may have been erected near to the church by the lord of the manor, primarily for the use of his family. But they are by no means peculiar to churchyards. In the days of horse transport they were a feature of public places, such as the market or town square. They might also be found where they could provide a service to travellers, perhaps as an aid to remounting at the top of a steep hill. Some examples extant may be medieval; they became more popular in the seventeenth century, were commonplace in the eighteenth and continued into the nineteenth. They were used for dismounting before the church service, and afterwards servants or grooms brought their masters' horses back to the steps. They would also have been used by country parsons who lived some distance from their churches, as well as those who did not for it was quite common for the vicar to stable his horse in the churchyard.

Stocks

The fact of the churchyard was always supposed to have a beneficial effect on criminals, even if only in the mind of the fugitive seeking sanctuary. Then they would at least be recognising the existence of a power for good which might encourage them to mend their ways. Implements of correction, such as the stocks and whipping posts, were sometimes sited near the church, no doubt so that the unfortunate contained in them might be influenced by the proximity of the consecrated ground. Some remain, reminders of the time when people were publicly displayed and abused for minor crimes. A few have now found their way into church porches. There are sets of stocks just outside several Cornish churchyards but at **Crantock** and **Feock** (a seven-holed set at the latter) they are inside. Small metal ones may be easily missed beyond the boundary wall at **Painswick**, Gloucestershire, and at **Market Overton**, Leicestershire, both stocks and whipping posts are nearby. **St Kew**, Cornwall, has a set in the church porch, and **Mobberley**, Cheshire, has one in the churchyard. A four-holed set is nearby at **Marden**, Kent, and the whipping post still stands by the churchyard gate at **Kingsley**, Staffordshire.

Lychgates

The main entrance to many churchyards is under a roofed structure called a lychgate. At **Troutbeck**, Cumbria, there are three and at **Stoke Poges**, Buckinghamshire, and **Bockleton**, Worcestershire, there are two. The name is derived from the Anglo-Saxon word *lich*, meaning corpse or body. The Prayer Book of 1549 required the priest to meet the deceased at the entrance to the churchyard and there conduct the beginning of the burial service. Poorer parishes which could not afford a gate might make do with flat steps at the entrance. There are several examples of these amongst Cornish churchyards, as at **Zennor** and **St Germoe**, which also has stone seats for the bearers. The gate at the point of entry into consecrated ground became known as the corpse gate. It provided rest and shelter for the bearers while they were waiting for the priest, and for all who were officiating in the early part of the service. Once the party was ready to move on, the parish bier was fetched from the church, where it was normally stored, and used to convey the body to the graveside. At **Walpole St Peter**, Norfolk, there is a 'hood' which could be used by the priest when officiating at the graveside in bad weather.

Some lychgates incorporated seats along their length. They were mostly of the bench type, made of stone, but there are two fine examples made of slate at **St Just-in-Roseland**, Cornwall. Other bench seats were made of wood. The corpse or coffin was rested on a three-legged coffin stool or, more usually, a wooden or stone oblong support called a coffin stone or corpse table. The structure at the entrance of **Mylor** churchyard, Cornwall, has a large granite stone flanked by stepping-stone stiles and stone seats, but the lychgate itself belongs to the twentieth century. A huge, roughly hewn granite boulder serves the purpose at **Luxulyan**, also in Cornwall. At **Bolney**, West Sussex, there is an example of a well made and proportioned coffin stone, long and narrow.

It is difficult to date lychgates accurately and they are frequently not made in the same materials as the church or the boundary walling. A few remain from the middle ages, their oak posts and supports pitted vertically and bleached by the elements to a silvery grey. Amongst those known to be medieval are **Anstey** and **Ashwell**, both in Hertfordshire; that at **Boughton Monchelsea**, Kent, is dated 1470 and is supposed to be the oldest in Britain although the one at **Limpsfield**, Surrey, is also ancient. Most date from the seventeenth and eighteenth centuries and were sometimes made out of the old timbers from the belfry or church roof. One such is at **Painswick**, Gloucestershire. Many are more recent memorials to individuals or groups of people. They may commemorate a vicar who restored the church or added to it by his own artistic talent, usually in the nineteenth century. They may recall some local worthy or benefactor, put up by his partner or family shortly after his death, or men from the parish who perished in the two world wars. Queen Victoria's jubilee occasioned a great number of lychgates. Those put up during or since Victorian times usually have a neat, brass plaque on them, bearing the essential details. On older ones, there may be religious texts or phrases cut into any plasterwork, or carved on horizontal beamwork or bargeboards. Vertical woodwork, if decorated at all, often included continuous floral motifs, and these are also to be found in the spandrels of any windows. **Betchworth**, Surrey, has a fine structure: wide and high with beautifully decorated bargeboards and a neat cross cut into the apex. There is a carved lychgate at **Battlefield**, Shropshire.

Most lychgates comprise a gabled roof of roofing tiles, wooden shingles, horizontal boards or thatch supported by an arrangement of openwork beams, braces, struts and vertical side members. Arch braces were frequently used in or comprised the sides of the structure where it was otherwise open, and the whole was executed in varying degrees of workmanship. In longitudinal section the roof frames tended to be simple king post, queen post or open roof truss types. Some have shaped or carved barge-boarding in the gables and in some the woodwork stands on a low wall base of stone or brick. The materials used in building the lychgate depended, before the construction of the canal system and the railways, on what was locally available.

The most common types of lychgate either have the roof ridge along the same axis as the passageway beneath or at right angles to it. In others, two roof ridges cross at right angles, inevitably seen as a symbolic effect where there was money to spare. **Clun**, Shropshire, has a four-gabled tiled roof. The gate at **Fleet**, Lincolnshire, is thatched. Sometimes the lychgate was built into a house at the point of entry. Others have rooms or dwellings above them which might have been used by the priest, as a schoolroom, parish room, library or store. Examples of such buildings are at **Long Compton**, Warwickshire, where the thatched room over the gate has a chimney and is a half-timbered construction in stone and brick, and **Bray**, Berkshire, where the room is of brick and timber. **Painswick**, Gloucestershire, has a plaster and timber building without gates but with bells carved on the bargeboards. The seventeenth century lychgate at **Wendron**, Cornwall, has a granite room above. Slate-hung upper rooms can also be seen at **Feock, Kenwyn** and **St Clement** in the same county. At **Ilsington**, Devon, the tiled upper room rests on pillars and is larger than the space beneath; it has leaded windows on two sides, a chimney and a niche which contains a statue. The gateways at **Hartfield**, East Sussex, and **Penshurst**, Kent, are both partly beneath the overhang of adjacent half-timbered medieval dwellings. That at **East Meon**, Hampshire, is roofed in stone and the wholly timber structure at **Horton**, Staffordshire, was built in 1902.

Occasionally one comes across a double lychgate with central support, and some lychgates are considerably wider than the majority. At **Bolney**, West Sussex, the roof has a wide sweep, like the wings of a bird. It reaches almost to the ground on either side and the structure has wide, curving braces and is supported by little stone walls. **Weston Turville** and **Chalfont St Giles**, both in Buckinghamshire, and **Burnsall**, North Yorkshire, have double revolving gates on a central post. They are controlled by the action of weights which are suspended to one side on chains over pulleys. The gates at **Friston**, East Sussex, **North Cerney**, Gloucestershire, and those of the sixteenth century at **Hayes**, Greater London (formerly Middlesex), swivel. The idea behind the centrally pivoted tapsel gate was the ease with which bearers could negotiate it. **Barsham**, Suffolk, has a fine thatched lychgate with timber-framed plasterwork above the lintel and a carved figure in oak on the centre post. **Clifton**, Derbyshire, is famed for its large clock in the gable over the lychgate, which also has little side lights, and at **Ightham**, Kent, is a double gate which also has a walkway to one side. At **Little Marlow**, Buckinghamshire, the double swinging lychgate is worked by a pulley. The beautifully rustic structure at **Anstey**, Hertfordshire, is tiled and to one side has a little brick room with a massive studded oak door. The roof is supported by huge oak posts. The gate at **Yateley**, Hampshire, is dated 1625 and that at **Rostherne**, Cheshire, 1640. **Staple**, Kent, is also seventeenth century work. There is an early nineteenth century example at **Llangadfan**, Powys, and the lychgate at **Seale**, Surrey, is dated 1863. **Overbury**, Worcestershire, is a building of note. It has a tiled roof and the pleasing arrangement of curved braces supported by a low, stone wall surrounds a large coffin stone, which has the proportions of a fine chest tomb.

The distribution of lychgates does not follow any pattern. One of the strangest examples is the combined lychgate and bell tower, a solid three-stage support for a steeply pitched belfry, which was put up at the entrance to the churchyard at **Great Bourton**, Oxfordshire, late in the nineteenth century. Interesting lychgates of later date include **Clifton Hampden**, Oxfordshire, built in 1844, **Downton**, Wiltshire, with its traceried bargeboarding dated 1892, and the art nouveau design of six years later at **Stackpole**, Dyfed. Also Victorian is the gate at **Bitteswell**, Leicestershire, while that at **Shere**, Surrey, was designed by Lutyens in 1901. At **Plumpton Wall**, Cumbria, the lychgate is a war memorial.

Boundaries and gates

If the churchyard does not have a lychgate it may be entered by a stile, a simple wooden or iron gate, or one with some device which admits people either singly or severally but keeps out animals. The ball and chain drop weight type such as may be seen at **Compton Greenfield**, Gloucestershire, was designed for that purpose, as were the 'Cornish' stiles, one of which can be seen at **Zennor**, Cornwall. There is a slate stile at **Morwenstow** in the same county. A tumble-gate allows entry into the churchyard at **Chedzoy**, Somerset, and **Fingest**, Buckinghamshire, has two seventeenth century wishing gates in its boundary wall. That of **Skenfrith**, Gwent, has an upright slab set back into the upper part of the wall and two stone steps below in order to reach it. At **Hungerford**, Berkshire, there is a five-barred stile.

Churchyard walls are worth investigating. **Seale**, Surrey, has an old stone wall around a sloping site. The upkeep of 'God's acre' was charged to the parish, which in medieval times had to enclose it and keep it in good order. They did so with boundary walls which prevented high churchyards from spilling on to surrounding lower ground, dry stone walls, yew hedges, and later brick walls, which matched the brick churches as at **Farley**, Wiltshire, and iron railings. Walls were built to keep out animals and contain the ground within. One of the most pleasing forms of walling is the ancient art of herringboning, such as may been seen at **Tintagel**, Cornwall. The name is derived from the pattern formed when layers of stones are placed diagonally, the horizontal rows alternately inclining to the left and right.

Some churchyard walls mark the extent of the parish boundary and will have in them a stone bearing the initials of the vicar. At **St Levan**, Cornwall, there is a stile and a cross in the wall. The most aesthetically pleasing are dry stone walls: layers of flat stones held together without mortar, by the pressure of one stone on another and the skill of the builders. Such walls are usually wider at the base than at the top, where they may be finished with coping stones. More sophisticated examples will include a filling of smaller stones between the outer layers and may be strengthened by occasional flat, through stones.

Where individuals were responsible for the upkeep of the boundary wall or fence, their initials may be inscribed on stones or cut into the fence supports. At **Herstmonceux**, East Sussex, each farm in the parish was responsible for the upkeep of a certain length of the churchyard fence, which accordingly is made up of a number of short runs with double posts. Fencing may have the names of individuals, farms or families carved on it. The wall at **Escomb**, Durham, is circular.

Pathways should not be taken for granted. Some are still only worn tracks. Others may be of gravel, pebbles, concrete, tarmac, flagstones and even headstones. Churchyards, particularly in towns, may lately have been turned into gardens of remembrance or have one associated with them, as at **Madron**, Cornwall. Others have, under deed of covenant, been made over to the local authority in part or whole for the purpose of maintaining a municipal precinct garden.

Wrought iron gates are worth more than a cursory glance. At one time almost all gates were low and made of oak. Provided they were put together with oak nails they would not rust and so had a long life. Ironwork occasioned much more by way of decoration, and many low gates will include an amount of simple scrollwork. There is nothing outside the church to match the quality of the interior screens, which is perhaps strange when one considers the fine ironwork village blacksmiths were fixing to doors as early as the thirteenth century. At all times dog rails were included in gates, irrespective of the material in which they were made.

Georgian gates might be highly decorated. At **Ashburton**, Devon, is a fine pair dated 1700. The gates at **Kendal**, Cumbria, are surmounted by a riot of bifurcated 'S' scrolls, a motif which also appears on the openwork gateposts. There is a frieze of horizontal 'S' scrolls, which is repeated on the double lock rail below, and each gate has ten verticals, the spaces between at the foot being further divided by an arrowhead dog rail. It embodies many of the motifs of the period, scrolls and strapwork having taken over from the sixteenth century arrangement of fleurs-de-lis or spike finials to the verticals, the whole joined by top and bottom rails. **Malpas**, Cheshire, has a fine set of gates made variously throughout the eighteenth century. From the same period are the two gateways with ornamental vases on the posts at **Wern**, Shropshire, and those at **Padstow**, Cornwall. The gateway at **Stapleford**, Nottinghamshire, is Victorian, as are also the fine iron gates at **Castlemartin**, Dyfed. Any lampholder set over or close by the churchyard gate is worthy of inspection, as it might prove to be the only remaining Victorian or Edwardian example thereabouts.

The first look around the churchyard

Occasionally one may find too many of what one does expect to see. There are two churches in one churchyard at **Swaffham Prior**, Cambridgeshire, **Evesham**, Worcestershire, **South Walsham** and **Reepham**, Norfolk, **Willingale**, Essex, and **Alvingham**, Lincolnshire. At **Trimley**, Suffolk, two churchyards, each with a church, adjoin each other. Some churchyards may have an area which is known by another name, perhaps that of a 'lost' village or nearby hamlet which never had a burial ground of its own.

Sometimes one must hack one's way through quite a jungle in order to get right up to the walls of the building. Elsewhere there will seem to be a ditch between the church and the churchyard. It is known as a *dry area* and in many cases became a necessary excavation in the nineteenth century. By that time a churchyard, which may have been in constant use for more than eight hundred years, would have risen high above the base of the walls. This could cause damp, and even structural problems. The walls had to be dug out at their base, dried out and given room and time to breathe. It is sometimes obvious where this has been done but the trench has since been allowed to fill in again. There will be a shallow depression.

It is well worth looking around the churchyard for objects which should not be there. There are two standing stones in the churchyard at **Rudston**, North Humberside. One of them, undoubtably of pagan origin and around which there is the customary superstitious legend, is over 25 feet (7.5 m) tall, with an unknown length underground. This chunk of gritstone was supposedly hurled at the church by the devil! There is a strange arrangement of two mutilated shafts flanking four semicircular stones in pairs in the churchyard at **Penrith**, Cumbria. Whilst legend ascribes the feature to the grave of a giant, the significance of the stones remains a mystery. A chance find in any churchyard could be a piece of medieval masonry such as you may never before have seen from so close. There is the frame of a medieval window in the churchyard at **Colyton**, Devon, and at **Iffley**, Oxfordshire, there is an ancient font bowl, although it is difficult to take one's eyes from the amazing decoration on the west front of the church! At **Stroud**, Gloucestershire, is the former top of the spire.

It is a good idea to walk right around the outside of a church before going in, to see what you can find both on the ground and in the walls of the building. Often you will see where bits were once built on or to a different height, discernible by the pitch of a former roof against a tower wall or by obviously blocked-up areas elsewhere. At **Dacre**, Cumbria, there are four lumps of stone, each shaped and carved to represent a bear in some activity with a cat. **Braunston**, Leicestershire, has a carved figure which appears to be a pagan fertility symbol and which may well have been the object of worship there before Christianity. **Naseby**, Northamptonshire, has a large copper ball which was once on top of the spire. What is thought to be a seventh century stone of unknown origin, inscribed *Noti noti*, lies at **St Hilary**, Cornwall, and several other churchyards in that county contain interesting inscribed stones of almost any age from the fifth century. Examples can be found at **Lanivet, Phillack** and **St Clement**. In one corner of the churchyard at **St Germoe** in the same county is a roofed seat known as St Germoe's chair. Nothing is known of its origin or use. At **St Levan**, Cornwall, there is a broken rock on which the saint is supposed to have rested when tired from fishing.

Most people will take a cursory glance around the churchyard and will notice anything which seems to be odd or out of place. Just as the interior of a small country church may sometimes be dominated by a huge tomb, so too may the churchyard have an obvious structure of note. Much of the pre-Conquest carving extant is fragmentary and rarely *in situ*. Anglo-Saxon carving, pieces of cross shafts and heads, tombstones and such like are more likely to be found displayed inside the church, or to be now built into internal or external walls. Your walk around the church will reveal anything of this nature which is on the outside; a popular position for ancient sculpture is at the east end beneath any east window in the chancel.

At **Brightling**, East Sussex, there is a pyramid to Mad Jack

Fuller; **Sharnbrook**, Bedfordshire, has an eighteenth century mausoleum with wrought iron gates and there is another at **Stone**, Staffordshire. **Madron**, Cornwall, has a mausoleum from the nineteenth century. **Bromham**, Wiltshire, has on the north side an overpowering Celtic cross to Thomas Moore and at **Dalham**, Suffolk, is Sir James Affleck's obelisk. There is another from the eighteenth century at **Kings Norton**, Leicestershire. An eccentric pyramidal monument in the churchyard at **Pinner**, Greater London (formerly Middlesex), topped by a casket lid and open at the base, has an empty coffin shape protruding from each side above the ground. There are also, here and there, detached mausoleums which are reputed to be of local saints, such as at **Holyhead** and **Llaneilian**, Anglesey, Gwynedd. At **Patshull**, Staffordshire, stands the stone statue of a man in armour.

Not all objects of interest in the churchyard are monuments. In one corner of the grounds at **Elkstone**, Gloucestershire, (a magnificent little Norman building) is a one-time priest's house which has fifteenth century windows. Small stone dwellings of this nature are common and may be seen close to the boundary wall in many places. There are stone buildings in the churchyard at **Downholme**, North Yorkshire. **Thaxted**, Essex, has an almshouse within the churchyard. The chancel arch from an earlier church is in the grounds at **Distington**, Cumbria, and **Bodmin**, Cornwall, has the ruins of a fourteenth century chapel. Parts of a former church, too, are at **Prestbury**, Cheshire. There is an early eighteenth century gabled house of brick in the churchyard at **Diseworth**, Leicestershire, and a brick building at **Chaddesley Corbett**, Worcestershire. The churchyard at **Uppingham**, Leicestershire, includes a school as well as some stonework from an earlier church. The site of the altar in the original church at **Hersham**, Surrey, is marked by a rectangular, commemorative stone in the grounds. There is an early nineteenth century school building in the churchyard at **Wraxall**, Avon. Occasionally little huts survive as reminders of the days of body snatching, when freshly deposited corpses were illegally dug up for use in experiments in the cause of medical science. It was the only way in which students of medicine could learn anatomy at first hand, and in order that they might develop their skills as surgeons they needed to practise on bodies which had not long been dead. The Anatomy Act, 1832, did away with the nefarious trade of the bodysnatchers. Perhaps the simplest deterrent to body snatching in areas where more costly items could not be afforded was to place a huge stone or boulder on the new graves. This would take several men to move it and it would stay in position until the corpse was no longer fit for medical purposes. Huge stones, now lying around a churchyard with seemingly no other purpose, may well have ensured that corpses were not disturbed in the past. Sometimes people did the job, and watchmen's boxes can be seen at **Wanstead**, Greater London (formerly Essex), and **Warblington**, Hampshire. At **Selborne** in the same county some of the graves were built with brick walls to discourage body snatching. **Henham**, Essex, has an iron cage, and the most common protection was the stone or iron vault known as a mort-safe. There is one at **Aberfoyle**, Scotland.

There are a number of dole stones. These are slabs — often the tops of chest tombs situated near the south porch — either made or set aside for administering a charity. Wealthy people sometimes bequeathed a sum of money so that bread could be bought and distributed to the local poor at their graveside on either the anniversary of their death or at some other appointed date during the year. There is one which seems to be purpose-built, decorated only by a cross at either end, at **Potterne**, Wiltshire. Another is in the churchyard at **Dundry**, Avon, and **Saintbury**, Gloucestershire, has an octagonal surface on an octagonal support for this purpose.

4. Churchyard crosses

Before the Reformation every churchyard included a freestanding stone cross. It signified the sanctity of consecrated ground. Many were destroyed by Cromwell's soldiers during the Civil War and the iconoclasts removed or broke up most of the heads which still bore sculptured images. The remains of churchyard crosses are still quite common, although they are mostly what was left after this destruction and desecration. In some instances subsequent levelling of the grounds included the churchyard cross in the overall plan to do away with the tombstones. As a result of all this, one may sometimes find sections of a cross lying together in the churchyard, set in concrete to give some idea of what the original was like, or even built into the fabric of the church. Not all those still standing may be in their original position, although post-Conquest ones are most likely to be. Others may have been brought from another place and several in close proximity may indicate that a collection has been made at some later date.

The earliest crosses were carved monoliths, put up close to pagan shrines, marking a place of former heathen worship. Some which are now in churchyards — especially in the south-west peninsula, where they are also to be seen by the roadside — may have marked routes, preaching stations, or even have been put up to show the extent of land ownership. The first Christian missionaries had their own crosses erected where they preached as well as at the places of former pagan activity which they converted to the new religion. Since these sites then became the first places of Christian worship and burial, the crosses extant from that period marked the sites before the first churches were built. The principle of the churchyard cross remained strong in areas under the influence of Celtic Christianity, having also been taken over in the north and north-east as a favourite form by the Danish invaders. However, new ideas for decoration came with the drive for the faith which spread from the south-east. Its art was inspired by that of the Mediterranean regions, as were those who came and those who were converted, by contact with this source. Celtic conversion was pushed to the edges of its former territory – the north, west and south-west – and in these strongholds the crosses were kept. Anglo-Saxon work is, in some areas, evident well into the eleventh century; in others it had become predominantly Anglo-Danish, such as at **Hauxwell**, North Yorkshire, where there is interlace, and **Prestbury**, Cheshire, where there is both interlace and animal carving.

Pre-Conquest crosses are not easy to date if there is no inscription. Shapeless carved stones were the forerunners of those which developed a cruciform outline and in Scotland the rough slab with a cross carved out of it continued to be popular. The designs on the crosses often originated from more than one source and were brought to a particular area by more than one invading element. Hence the distribution of crosses of similar type and decoration may indicate one or other of two main things. The first is the route taken by an invading element or the extent of its territorial influence. The second is the fact of its apparent stability and authority, allowing a school of art to flourish in the region. To put an accurate date on a cross which is without inscription one needs to know the artistic influences at work in the area at the time, who brought them and for how long they were there. As they were overtaken in turn, different areas admitted a succession of designs on their crosses and there were regional characteristics. Whorls, scrolls, other geometric patterns, plaiting, interlacing, vine scrolls, human heads, leaf motifs, animals and figurework appeared variously on both the heads and the shafts, and much of it was stylised.

The standard shape for the early crosses outside the south-west consisted of a tall shaft with a comparatively small head. In the south-west the shafts were often dumpy in appearance and crudely incised as, for example, at **St Dennis**, Cornwall. The tallest of the Cornish type, although not the most ornamental, is in **Mylor** churchyard. There are several in the churchyard at **St Levan**. Elsewhere churchyard crosses might be circular in cross section, as at **Masham**, North Yorkshire, **Brailsford**, Derbyshire, and **Wolverhampton**, West Midlands, or rectangular. Occasionally they were constructed with both circular and rectangular sections in the same shaft, as at **Ilam**, Staffordshire, where there are two crosses, and **Beckermet St Bridget** and **Gosforth**, both in Cumbria. The cross at **Wolverhampton**, of the ninth century, is some 14 feet (4 m) high and exuberantly decorated in sections, forming an all-over arrangement of wild motifs and leaf shapes. **Brailsford**, of the eleventh century, has interlacing and figurework. The tapering shaft at **Stapleford**, Nottinghamshire, is also decorated in sections and has dividing banding; it includes interlacing and a face. The tenth century example at **Sproxton**, Leicestershire, has interlacing and a beast.

A fusion of both these designs can be seen in the fragments of two crosses at **Sandbach**, Cheshire. They include interlacing, vine scroll, beasts and religious tableaux. The ninth century stump at **Bakewell**, Derbyshire, also has a vine scroll and animals, as well as human figures.

There are comparatively few pre-Conquest crosses in churchyards, although Cornwall, taken in isolation, might seem to disprove this statement, but the land of so many obscure saints, setting up preaching crosses all over the place, can hardly be considered typical. One can scarcely enter a churchyard in Cornwall without coming across an ancient cross or at least a stone around which there is usually speculation if not legend. Some of these 'crosses' were almost certainly ancient stones of some pre-Christian religious significance, later put to the service of Christianity by some reshaping or additional carving. Many crosses in Cornish churchyards may have interlace or plait decoration and inscriptions in Roman transitional or Hiberno-Saxon characters. A comprehensive listing includes **Cardinham, Feock, Lamorran, Lanhydrock, Lanivet, Lanteglos by Fowey, Launceston, Lostwithiel, Mylor, Padstow, Par, Phillack, Porthilly, Roche, St Allen, St Clement, St Dennis, St Ives, St Juliot, St Mawgan, St Neot, St Teath, Sancreed** and **Wendron**. There are pillar stones in the churchyards of **Gulval, Lanivet, Lanteglos by Camelford, Lewannick, Phillack** and **South Hill**, and coped stones at **Lanivet, Phillack, St Buryan** and **St Tudy**. An interesting comparison can be made between the relatively conservative and rustic work being done on churchyard crosses in Cornwall and the barbaric and thematic examples being put up in the north of England at the same time. At **St Buryan** the cross head of the eighth century which shows the crucifixion is fixed on a plinth, and at **Zennor** there are two which are even older. There is a very rustic example at **Roche**, two at **St Juliot**, one reputed to be sixth century at **Altarnun** and no less than five at **Sancreed**. Of these, one has a very early inscription, possibly reused, and another is of the tenth century. Others of interest are at **Phillack** and **Lanivet**. Cornwall, like the north-west and also the west coast of Wales, has a predominance of the wheelhead type. Elsewhere a ninth century example can be seen at **Rolleston**, Staffordshire; there is another at **Dearham**, Cumbria, and the tenth century example at **Gosforth** in the same county is about 15 feet (4.5 m) tall. The extent of the carving on any cross depended on the materials used, and its present condition indicates whether or not the material weathered well. Most were done in local stone and some of the finest examples extant were carved in the granite of the far west. The exception to this is at **Breage**, Cornwall, where is to be found the only sandstone preaching cross in the country.

Cumbria has fine examples of Norse, Danish and Celtic art in its churchyards. Scrolls, two, three and four strand plaiting, interlace and knotwork provided the earliest decoration. Particularly good are the crosses, cross shafts and hogback tombstones. The figurework of Christ, the Virgin Mary, saints and biblical tableaux, which were a feature of Northumbrian work from the seventh century, persisted as favourite decoration for churchyard crosses until the sixteenth century. The best cross shaft stands over 14 feet (4.3 m) tall in **Bewcastle** churchyard. Made of sandstone in the seventh century and of the same style as **Ruthwell**, Dumfries-shire, the headless shaft remains. It is boldly carved with several motifs and panelled on each of its four sides with figures, vine scroll, knotwork, inhabited scrolls, leaves, birds and animals. It also includes the earliest extant Saxon sundial. The surrounding tombstones have beautifully shaped heads and, although centuries apart, provide a fine setting for the cross shaft. The eighth century cross at **Ruthwell** is 18 feet (5.5 m) tall. Norse and Christian themes are together depicted on the slender and complete cross in **Gosforth** churchyard. The ninth century cross at **Ireton** has panels of interlacing and knotwork, done in a barbaric style. The inhabited vine scroll which was a feature of churchyard crosses in this region was a combination of vine scroll from the Mediterranean regions and animals and birds from Germanic origins, adopted and adapted into fine carvings.

The appearance of beasts on crosses is of Scandinavian origin, and most are to be found in the north. The influence is heavy at **Heversham**, Cumbria, where there are the remains of the ninth century shaft with scrollwork, fruit, birds and beasts, and at **Kirkby Stephen**, where the fragment has figurework and interlacing. The same is true of **Burton-in-Kendale**, where there is also scrollwork. Other interesting late northern pre-Conquest crosses or remains can be found at **Eyam** and **Hope**, Derbyshire, **Leek** and **Checkley**, Staffordshire, **Dacre**, Cumbria, **Heysham** and **Halton**, Lancashire, **Winwick**, Cheshire, and **Whalley**, Lancashire. The last is a round shaft with chamfered edges. There are three Anglo-Saxon cross shafts at **Ilkley**, West Yorkshire. The churchyard at **Creeton**, Lincolnshire, has two, one with interlace and the other including incised crosses. Although now inside the church, the two joined fragments of a shaft, _c_ 1000, at **Nunburn-**

holme, North Humberside, should be mentioned. The decoration on it includes figurework and animals. Anglo-Saxon work is present in the churchyard shafts at **Alstonfield**, Staffordshire, which include the head of a serpent, and the three at nearby **Checkley**, which have figurework. There are both figures and animals at **Masham**, North Yorkshire. There is figurework at **Somersby**, Lincolnshire, a base at **Hornby**, Lancashire, and some fine work at **Heysham**, Lancashire, depicting a gabled building with windows, figures, busts and scrollwork. The shaft at **Rothley**, Leicestershire, is 12 feet (3.7 m) tall. There is interlace at **Bromborough**, Merseyside. Another fine Celtic cross is in the churchyard at **Nevern**, Dyfed, and was made in the tenth century. It is a 13 foot (4 m) tall wheelhead, decorated with panelled plait and interlace. On later pre-Conquest crosses there was a gradual decline in the old-style decoration and a move towards more extensive Christian figurework, especially on the head. At **Broadway**, Somerset, there are two figures on the tapering shafts put up in the fourteenth century.

For most of the middle ages the churchyard cross was the single memorial to almost all who had ever been buried thereabouts. It invariably marked the true centre of the churchyard at a point to the east of a processional path midway between the main entrance to the churchyard and the south porch of the church, and it was used as a station on days of prayer and thanksgiving. Particularly, these were Rogation Day, Corpus Christi and Palm Sunday. Such an important part did the decorated cross play on Palm Sunday that it was frequently referred to as the 'Palm Cross'. It also played a part in the secular life of the community, being the point from which public announcements could be made. At **Alkborough**, South Humberside, the smooth, strange shape of the cross shaft is the result of its constant use for honing weapons, scythes and other instruments.

The mounted shaft type of cross predominated and the remains extant are mainly of this kind. In its complete form it consisted of steps, base (plinth or socket), shaft, capital (or knop) and head. What tends to remain, if a restored head has not been added to a new shaft, are steps, base and a short length of shaft.

There may be between one and six steps made of individual stones, forming a structure which is either round, square, rectangular, hexagonal or octagonal. The steps diminish upwards in surface area and sometimes the treads are continued over the risers as a roll moulding or set-off. Particularly in the fourteenth century one step of each set might be carved as panels on each of its faces, but rarely was such decoration lavished on more than one tier. There is a good fourteenth century cross at **North Cerney**, Gloucestershire, and one from the fifteenth century at **Tattershall**, Lincolnshire.

The foot of the shaft was received in a socket or plinth, some of which are comparatively tall. These either follow the shape of the steps or are square, occasionally with chamfered vertical edges. They are more inclined to have decoration, ranging from plain thirteenth century trefoils to the panelled quatrefoils and heraldry of the fourteenth century. The majority of shafts are square in plan and taper upwards. They often have chamfered edges terminating in typical stops. Most are plain but some have minor carving or figurework along their length, the latter more often at the point of contact with the base. A niche or recess, occasionally canopied, was sometimes built into one side of the shaft or socket, to hold either a sculpture or a monstrance or the pyx on ceremonial occasions. An example of this is at **Great Malvern**, Worcestershire. One which includes figurework within a niche on the shaft is at **Crowcombe**, Somerset, a cross with a heavy floriated knop.

There is sometimes a capital between the shaft and the head; otherwise there may be no division at all or the two may be separated by a single roll. Capitals tend to be squat, a shallow row of minor floral motifs between the roll and a flatter abacus. Some have volutes or stiff leaf forms virtually corbelled out from the head above, which may also have minor decoration on the underside. The heads were themselves either flat-topped or gabled, two or four sided, and in many instances surmounted by a cross. It is these which commanded the attention of the iconoclasts in the churchyard whilst they were engaged on similar destruction elsewhere in the church. Much of what we see today has been heavily restored and the remains of some old crosses have since been converted into sundials. The two-sided heads usually had a rood on one side and a figure sculpture of the Virgin and Child on the other. Four-sided heads depicted these amongst other sculptured figurework and decoration on all faces – canopies, finials, buttresses.

There is a complete although restored medieval cross of the gabled type at **Ampney Crucis**, Gloucestershire, and another at **Somersby**, Lincolnshire. The fourteenth century cross at **Tyberton**, Herefordshire, is also gabled, with the figure of Christ on the cross on one side, the Virgin and Child on the other. Here the 10 foot (3 m) shaft is tapered and has elongated spurs at the foot, the whole being set on a huge base block. Cross shafts known to have been made in the fourteenth century include the one with a lantern head and niches at **Ashleworth**, Gloucestershire; **Bishop's Lydeard**, Somerset, which has figurework; **Higham Ferrers**, Northamptonshire, where there is an amount of floral decoration and minor decorative motifs; **Ross-on-Wye**, Herefordshire; and **Blakemere** in the same county. Other interesting medieval crosses include **St Mawgan**, Cornwall, **Chewton Mendip**, Somerset, **Cricklade** and **Bremhill**, Wiltshire, **North Hinksey**, Oxfordshire,

Edlesborough, Buckinghamshire. On an artificial, grassy mound to the west of the village and on the edge of the Chilterns, the church is a dominating landmark against the skyline.

Hawkshead, Cumbria. Beloved and romantically described by Wordsworth, the church is in an elevated position near the Cumbrian mountains and Esthwaite Water and commands fine views.

Robeston Wathen, Dyfed. Typical of the area in both design and building material, the tower is heavy and unbuttressed with a projecting upper stage.

Wanborough, Wiltshire. Eroded, mossy tombstones tilt here, on the north side, and a goat nibbles at the wilderness, which in summer is a haven for wildlife in this typical country village. The church is noted for its hexagonal lantern and spire.

(Left) Shere, Surrey. Note the old lamp and the pleasing way in which the roofs and gables group together and lead the eye towards the spire, all perfectly linked by the foliage. The lychgate is by Lutyens, 1901.
(Below) Clapton-on-the-Hill, Gloucestershire. Looking through the horseshoe gate towards the twelfth-century church, which has an endearing little capped turret on the east end of the nave.

Ashwell, Hertfordshire. The double lychgate was put up in the fifteenth century. The light, open church has graffiti on the tower.

Weston Turville, Buckinghamshire. Here the lychgate is more a pair of covered boundary gates on a central pivot, controlled by weighted chains which run over pulleys to one side.

Whalley, Lancashire. The slender late pre-Conquest cross shaft includes figurework and knotwork.

Masham, North Yorkshire. A 7 foot (2 m) four-tier section of a ninth-century Anglo-Saxon cross; it includes figurework, animals and tableaux. J. C. Ibbetson, the artist, is buried in the grounds.

Westbury-on-Severn, Gloucestershire. One of the county's two detached towers, set in a large churchyard. Originally a thirteenth-century watch tower, it is earlier than the church and is topped by a tall spire from the fourteenth century.

East Wellow, Hampshire. The memorial to Florence Nightingale, who spent her youth at nearby Embly Park. The church is notable for its thirteenth-century wall paintings.

Malmesbury, Wiltshire. A typical mixture of memorials, spanning many centuries and well spaced in the extensive grounds. The open ogee arch is unusual. Note the lichen and creeper.

Swinbrook, Oxfordshire. Outside are the seventeenth- and eighteenth-century roll top tombs to the Pleydells by local masons, and the twentieth-century graves of Unity and Nancy Mitford. Inside, the Fettiplace effigies are stacked on shelves in the chancel.

Heare Lies
Neare Two of
my children Dea
re Robert aged
10
2 years mon Mary
2 Days 1668

Thame, Oxfordshire. A riverside church noted for its medieval altar tombs. The simple decoration and indifferent design of this tombstone is a marked contrast.

Hatfield, Hertfordshire. One of a few wooden graveboards; note the poppy-headed finials to the posts. The churchyard, on a hill, is entered through iron gates, made in 1710 and brought from St Paul's Cathedral.

Llandyssul, Dyfed. Typical Victorian designs in Welsh slate, classical and sombre with copy-book inscriptions, in a churchyard on the banks of the Teifi.

IN REMEMBRANCE
OF
EDITH NELLIE WILBY
WHO DEPARTED THIS LIFE JULY 17TH 1908
AGED 17 YEARS

FORBEAR, DEAR FRIENDS, TO MOURN AND WEEP
WHILST SWEETLY IN THE DUST I SLEEP.
THIS TOILSOME WORLD I'VE LEFT BEHIND
A GLORIOUS CROWN I HOPE TO FIND

IN REMEMBRANCE
OF
OUR DEAR MOTHER
RACHEL WILBY
WHO DIED DEC 19TH 1932
AGED 84 YEARS
SAFE IN GODS OWN KEEPING
JUST BEYOND OUR SIGHT
AT REST

(Above) Great Tey, Essex. Functional memorials, cast and painted.

CECIL
DAY LEWIS
1904–1972
Poet Laureate

Shall I be gone long?
For ever and a day.
To whom there belong?
Ask the stone to say.
Ask my song.

(Left) Stinsford, Dorset. In the same churchyard is the heart of Thomas Hardy, whose ashes are in Westminster Abbey.

Ombersley, Worcestershire. The Sandys mausoleum, made out of the heavy embattled chancel of old St Andrew's church, to the south of the present one.

Hampton, Greater London (formerly Middlesex). The strange late eighteenth-century monument to John Grey of Dominica.

Little Ouseburn, North Yorkshire. Henry Thompson's late eighteenth-century mausoleum: a domed Palladian rotunda with frieze supported by Tuscan columns.

Croxton, Cambridgeshire, and **Ightfield**, Shropshire, which has quatrefoils at the base and figures on the angles; at **Highley**, Shropshire, the shaft has cable moulding and figurework.

The fifteenth century cross at **Iron Acton**, Avon, is worthy of note, if badly mutilated, as is **Chewton Mendip**, Somerset, and at **Castle Hedingham**, Essex, is one of the twelfth century, restored. **Ombersley**, Worcestershire, although put up in the fifteenth century, has the addition of an eighteenth century ball finial. At **Rampisham**, Dorset, there is figurework of the sixteenth century in tableaux on the base. The medieval shaft at **Iffley**, Oxfordshire, received a new top in the nineteenth century, and at **Ombersley**, Worcestershire, is a cross which has been attended to at several times. The medieval base of four worn steps is set on a circular plinth. The upper step has quatrefoils and the head is from the seventeenth century. Later crosses of note may be seen at **Sulham**, Berkshire, and **Bournemouth** (St Peter's), Dorset.

5. Memorials

Burials

Although the years of Danish invasion had a limiting influence on church building, especially in those areas most vulnerable to attack and occupation, some northern churchyards have sets of fine Anglo-Danish tombstones of a particular type. Known as *hogbacks*, these low stones are wide in relation to their height, with a curved upper surface terminating in a gable at either end. The general shape is reminiscent of the Viking House of the Dead and the inward-looking animal carvings at the ends may have some significance in warding off evil spirits. The stones are highly decorated throughout. At the top there is usually a frieze of some minor decorative motif, repeated in continuous order and following the curve of the stone. Beneath may be vertical or horizontal bands of knotwork, plaiting or running spirals, or there may be scenes depicting Scandinavian mythology. Examples may be seen at **Brompton-in-Allerton**, North Yorkshire, **Lowther, Aspatria, Gosforth** and **Penrith**, Cumbria, and **Heysham**, Lancashire. Similarly, there are coffin-shaped or hogback coped stones to be found in whole or part elsewhere, notably in the far west at **St Buryan, St Tudy, Lanivet** and **Phillack** in Cornwall. The one at Lanivet has beasts and knotwork, whilst St Tudy includes scrollwork and interlace by way of decoration. **Muncaster**, Cumbria, has Saxon and Viking stones.

The Anglo-Saxons sometimes buried their dead in wooden coffins but it was not until early in the seventeenth century that wooden coffins made of flat boards came into general use. Some churches can furnish examples of pre-Conquest coffin panels, slabs or lids: **St Tudy**, Cornwall, **Wirksworth**, Derbyshire, **Dearham**, Cumbria, and **St Minver**, Cornwall, where some pre-Christian coffins were found in the churchyard. There are Saxon grave covers at **Kirkoswald**, Cumbria. Throughout the middle ages most people were interred in only a shroud, tied head and foot. It was supported to the graveside by the parish bier and placed straight into the ground. A sprig of rosemary for remembrance (also symbolically used at weddings) or yew foliage as a symbol of immortality was sometimes put into the grave.

Tradition continued the Norman precedent of beginning burials at one side of the grounds, working across, then starting again. Consequently in the course of time people were buried one on top of the other. The bodies of some who died away from home might be rendered down and only the bones returned for burial. This method of interment means that care should be taken, in the cause of churchyard archaeology, to note and record anything from the lower layers when new graves are being dug.

Churchyard burials during the twelfth and thirteenth centuries were sometimes made in rectangular stone coffins, let into the ground to their upper edges and covered with stone slabs. These ledgers were thick and either rectangular or coffin-shaped in cross plan, flat or gently coped. They included no inscription and were otherwise plain or bore an incised Latin or floriated cross. Priests, knights and others with a trade of note within the community might also have a subsidiary carving in low relief, indicating the nature of their calling. A knight, for example, might be remembered by an heraldic shield. Gradually the basic cross became more floral, assuming leaf form decoration, which developed as naturalistic foliage. The next step was a crudely cut outline of the deceased, forerunner of the fully developed effigy within the church. When the flat coffin slab became the elevated ledger of the chest tomb, its potential as a surface for embellishment was not realised, such being confined to its vertical faces. Later coffin slabs were sometimes put up in conjunction with plain headstones and footstones. However, individual churchyard monuments seem to have declined in popularity by the fourteenth century. There may have been widespread disillusionment and disbelief in the possibility of the resurrection.

Theoretically the shroud had to be made of wool from 1667 to 1814, in an attempt to help the declining wool trade, which had been responsible for such magnificent church building. There was an indifferent response to the original Act and it was amended in 1679. This new Act required that a certificate be produced for every burial before the service took place. Even so, it was 1696 before this was rigorously enforced.

People could not buy plots as they can today and the closest many got to interment in a coffin was temporary residence in the one which belonged to the parish. Consequently no one could feel that they actually owned any part of the churchyard. As true religious feeling declined within the church, so too did the respect towards those interred within the grounds. People continued to be placed one above the other and the ground level of many churchyards rose to that of the top of any surrounding wall, or higher. Sextons removed the bones from previous burials in order to make way for new ones and collected them together into crypts or charnel houses. Gravediggers stole the fixtures from the coffins for resale and, as the graveyards became so overcrowded, private individuals opened up plots and crammed in bodies at an alarming rate. Records from the early nineteenth century mention the stench which emanated from graveyards as a result of so much decaying flesh so shallowly buried. Gravestones which have been reused can be seen at **Heptonstall**, West Yorkshire.

Headstones

The headstones of churchyard graves are the counterparts of the wall tablets within the church, although they are in no way as well preserved nor do they give as much information. They became popular after the Reformation and by the end of the sixteenth century many more people could afford to buy separate plots and decided that their last resting place on earth should be marked in some way. Where materials allowed freedom to the craftsmen's skills, the period from about 1700 to 1850 saw some outstanding monumental masonry. The best headstones and tombs are Georgian. Headstones were made in local stone to begin with, and later artificial stone, slate, polished 'marbles' or cast iron. Where local stone was used because it was plentiful, the material might have been the same as that in the walls of the church, obtained from the same quarry. Iron gravestones appear in areas where there was always little freestone and iron smelting had gone on from the earliest times, such as in Sussex and Kent. Everywhere else the material used was, for hundreds of years, the easiest to hand. Transportation of stone was a costly business, even by waterway, before the coming of the railways made it much more practicable. It was laborious, time-consuming and hazardous. But with better communications, the business of the local mason using local stone declined as shiny white marble and firms of monumental masons increased in popularity.

Inscriptions were traditionally carved into a vertical surface of the headstone, although locally some might be affixed on metal or terracotta plates. An older headstone in which there was no further local personal interest was sometimes recut with the details of another person and used to mark a more recent interment. The style of the inscriptions, and that of the stones generally, varies considerably between areas. Groups of headstones in a particular district often show the unmistakable hand of a single sculptor. A signature may occasionally reveal the identity of a craftsman from long ago. Local craftsmen were, especially in the more rural areas, almost entirely responsible for this work until later in the nineteenth century, a time when tombstones were being given comparatively little ornamentation or decoration.

All headstones are subject to weathering. The softer stones may well have originally taken the best carving but are now in the poorest condition. Air pollution and industrial grime have turned others from grubby brown to black as soot. The more porous the original material, the less likely it is to have withstood the elements and not been badly eroded.

Most headstones are single although some double plots may be identified by stones which are twice the normal width, each with two shaped heads. Just as materials and standards of lettering varied, so too the size and shape of headstones developed regional characteristics. In some areas they always remained small, perhaps no more than between 2 and 3 feet (600-900 mm) tall like the early medieval ones, or even less. Individual churchyards show their own preferences for both size and the shape of the head. Whichever sort of headstone is found, the inscription may commemorate one or two people or even whole families. Early ones were thick in relation to their height. They increased in size and diminished in thickness. Some headstones in the exposed far west had to be buttressed against the prevailing winds. Graves may also have smaller footstones, usually giving only initials and date. Care should be taken not to confuse these with small or early headstones. Other graves may be enclosed in bedheads or graveboards.

At the beginning of the seventeenth century there was little decoration on headstones. They were fairly small and thick, mostly of stone although some of the common shapes were still being made in wood. The heads were flat except where a scroll formed the shoulders, perhaps flanking a winged angel's head, symbolic of the departing soul. Early seventeenth century angels were lean-featured. Their wings tended to stick awkwardly out from their heads in the place of ears but with the shape of handlebar moustaches. There are thousands of examples of sad, lone angels crudely cut on seventeenth and early eighteenth century tombstones by rural craftsmen. But the influence of classical art was to change their lean appearance into healthy, well fed cherubs, trumpeting their victory over death and winging into the hereafter with a smile and a tune.

The general carving as well as the lettering was decisive, bold and crude with little attention to layout. Roman capitals were common but lower-case characters were also used, often two or more contracted, and letters with tails ended in loops or hooks. If the word at the end of the line could not be completed because of lack of space it might be abbreviated, carried on to the next line or finished above. The letters were uneven: neither straight up and down nor sloping in the same direction as each other, but variously. Words were run together without spacing and only the width of the stone imposed any constraint on the mason's layout. If the text had a border any word which could not be contained within it at the end of a line might continue over the border into what we would call the margin. It all seems to have got worse before it got better, or perhaps it was just poor local standards of lettering which produced inscriptions with insertions above the line, at right angles to the rest of the text or squashed on the end of the line in tiny characters. In the seventeenth century early attempts at italic forms were made, although these were more effective when done on slate. In other instances a potentially strong line might be marred by the soft or brittle texture of the material into which it was cut.

By the middle of the century the top of the stone was being shaped to admit an angel's head in the hood, or else the shoulders were so carved to curve around one in each corner or spandrel, retaining the scroll from the centre of the piece to the outer edges. The text was sometimes cut on a cartouche shape, then becoming popular for internal monuments, perhaps surmounted by a skull or urn. The influence of classical art was adding decorative motifs such as swags, garlands, fruit and flowers. The calligraphic style of lettering quickly became popular and was applied with some interesting effect. This was especially well done in the slate producing areas, for the italic swirls looked particularly impressive cut sharply into the dark, impermeable background of slate. The faces of angels as well as their wings also took on a calligraphic style and lettering generally became smaller, more controlled and decorative. By the latter half of the century the headstone resembled a plaque surrounded by all manner of classical designs, pilasters, columns and even pediments. **Shangton** and **Swithland**, Leicestershire, have particularly attractive collections of seventeenth century headstones.

However, in the matters of decorative quality and lettering one can only generalise. In some rural areas the eighteenth century began with work hardly better than fifty years or so before and certainly the classical influences, which were elsewhere being put to considerable use as the century began, were slower in showing. Different styles of lettering were coming into fashion at the start of the century, which was remarkable for the great variety of forms and styles achieved by masons, sculptors and engravers. They used and adapted ancient designs, incised and in relief. But they were rarely used in juxtaposition on the same headstone. Individual words were given embellishment, or more commonly the tails of key letters were continued into scrolls. The witty or droll remarks by way of epitaphs gradually gave way to short, stereotyped phrases such as 'at rest' and 'at peace'. The main area of decoration on the headstone became the upper part, which in some cases took up the largest portion of the stone's surface. Whole biblical scenes might be carved. They were often interspersed with or surmounted by the winged heads of angels or cherubs. Skulls, too, remained popular.

The increase in the desire for individually commemorated graves provided a greater need for the skills of the local mason, and work by whole families in specific areas became more frequent and therefore more obvious. Individuality as regards the type of ornamentation within the framework of prevailing taste increased. So too did the styles of lettering. There were still some contractions of words but layout was generally much better. Before the letters took on decorated forms they were, for a while, extremely clear and simple in their various forms. Angels discovered bodies and drifted across headstones, blowing their trumpets. And, with the fashion for classical drapery, some very voluptuous angels they sometimes were. By the late eighteenth century they were taking their places as the centrepieces of tableaux amidst shells, urns, drapery and symbolism. Angels' features grew more cherubic and feathery wings grew out of their shoulders. The urn predominated, usually in the head of the stone, which also had swags, fruit and flowers. Some beautiful examples were now carved in slate with the decoration – even of pedimented obelisks – done in relief, with symmetrical designs and lettering. What was elsewhere sculpted out of freestone was, in the slate regions, beautifully engraved and it is there also that the great variety of lettering can still be seen at its best. At **Narborough**, Leicestershire, there is a good collection of tall eighteenth and nineteenth century headstones made out of Swithland slate, decorated with classical motifs in relief. The Wealden iron industry produced grave slabs in that material, such as are to be seen at **Cowden**, Kent. And at **Madeley**, Shropshire, there are nineteenth century cast iron tombs. A series of pretty terracotta plaques appeared on headstones in Sussex and there, as well as in Kent, one finds a number of strangely headed stones overloaded with skulls. Some foreign 'marbles' were imported and composite stone became popular. Most old churchyards which have not been cleared can provide examples of eighteenth century headstones, but there are some attractive ones at **Hambledon** and **Hayling Island**, Hampshire, **Cley-next-the-Sea** and **Blakeney**, Norfolk, **Narborough**, Leicestershire, **Inglesham**, Wiltshire, and **Shilton**, Oxfordshire.

Religious feeling in the nineteenth century dictated that not only should everyone have a separate plot, but that each should be decently commemorated by a headstone or some other memorial. It had been relatively easy to move aside old bones and insert new coffins until the ground was so overcrowded that the uppermost were very shallow graves indeed, and the stench unbearable. But headstones were another problem altogether. They did not allow cramming or facilitate surreptitious clearances; they were permanent as far as the Victorians were concerned. Private burial grounds had come into being and the problems there were very acute. One has a vision of gravediggers collecting together old bones, depositing them in charnel houses, perhaps reburying them; of bodysnatchers engaged in their nefarious activities helped, no doubt, by the shallowness of some interments, and private 'developers' commanding good prices for what must have been fairly indecent burials.

The reaction to all this was the Victorian desire to emphasise the ownership, sanctity and privacy of the grave plot. This they achieved from the mid nineteenth century with kerbs, cast iron rails and veritable fences. The work of the local man with his regional peculiarities of style and rustic lettering gave way to the standard typefaces and designs offered in the catalogues of the large monumental masonry firms. They were as varied as the materials used, deeply and perfectly cut, some leaded and others with shaded and three-dimensional effects. The craftsmen experimented widely with their own styles of lettering, and headstones of this period often include many different kinds in the same piece of text, and even slight alternatives for individual letters within the same line. The most popular type of headstones were the depressed, pointed type based loosely on the lancet and the symbolic triple head which represented the Holy Trinity. A line of small motifs invariably followed the shape of the head, which was otherwise fairly plain except, perhaps, for the prevailing classical urn. Fruit and flowers were always popular and they – and figurework – now became much more naturalistic. Inscriptions were all important, often surrounded by simple and formal items of classical architecture. There were obelisks and casket-shaped monuments, much statuary, as well as the ubiquitous freestanding cross – all usually in white marble. Some came from Italy, and there were a number of native 'marbles' (see chapter 9) but there was a particular vogue in the churchyard for Scottish and Cornish granite.

Epitaphs are those words of wit and wisdom, poignancy and sadness, in rhyme or prose, which people have long used on memorials to themselves and others, reflections on their life, death and afterlife. Epitaphs comprise a field of study of their own and will not be discussed in detail here. There is a companion volume to this (*Discovering Epitaphs* by Geoffrey N. Wright) which describes the subject and gives many examples. Whilst a good many are unique and there are some gems amongst them, a great number are universal in spirit, if not almost word for word.

Graveboards
An alternative to the headstone, especially in the south-east,

where there was little good local freestone, was the wooden graveboard. These covered the grave lengthways. They were long, horizontal pieces of board supported at either end by low wooden uprights which might themselves be terminated in a poppyhead finial. Some had chamfered upper edges along their length on which an inscription could be cut, but they were frequently painted white and lettered in black paint on a horizontal surface. Graveboards may be difficult to find, for, being made of wood – albeit oak or teak – they eventually rotted with age. However, even outside wooden memorials usually outlast local interest in the person they are commemorating. They are less expensive and could more easily be removed and disposed of if necessary. Another advantage of this kind of memorial is that it could be designed to be easily removed when the grass was being cut, to be replaced when the mowing was done. The current practice of putting plots close together side by side makes it difficult to use even a pair of shears between the tombstones once they have been erected, let alone a mower.

Graveboards are usually located, in those churchyards which have them, in the most inconspicuous parts. Those who could afford it soon preferred stone tombs and memorials even if they had to import the material into their area. The distribution of types of memorial within the churchyard is evidence of a definite class structure in its use. Those who could only afford a wooden board between two uprights when a choice was available – and painted instead of carved – were tucked into out-of-the-way corners of the grounds. The legends on most old graveboards are no longer decipherable. Their use was particularly widespread in Surrey, Kent and the area of the Chilterns. Some which may still be read – nineteenth century examples with chunky finials on the supporting posts – are in the churchyards at **Burstow** and **Mickleham**, Surrey.

Chest tombs

Chest or table tombs originated from the wooden shrines which were erected around the remains of local saints, although the idea was not developed in community use for some centuries. Who with the money for a fine raised tomb would have chosen to put it outside when the altar tomb, the internal equivalent, provided a psychologically more comfortable alternative? It was also more likely to remain in a pristine condition and in the same place. The hollow chest arrangement above graves in the churchyard was a side effect of the altar tomb concept of a rectangular box designed to form the high base for a recumbent effigy. In the churchyard the effigy was always omitted, and the only likenesses of the deceased which were possibly attempted may have been the few portrait busts carved on the ends of some chests in the eighteenth century. Even these were more by way of symmetrical decoration at a time when the ends of many chest tombs were being similarly treated to the surfaces of headstones. The tops of chest tombs always remained above the level of grass and weeds, and they were certain to stand out from even a forest of headstones. Yet as they are hollow, they are liable to collapse through the action of stress, soil erosion, age and the encroachment of roots. Care should be taken when close to chest tombs and monuments which have derived from them and which now appear to be in an unsafe condition. Many are covered with lichen – which is not to their detriment unless it has rendered inscriptions unreadable – or overgrown with ivy and creeper, which may have all but obliterated any wording or decoration which was once on the surfaces of older monuments, and the most that may be said in its favour is that it looks pretty.

Early chest tombs were rectangular stone boxes with little if any decoration and no inscription. In the fourteenth century the sides, like those of other items of church furniture such as fonts, were worked into a resemblance of window tracery. Cusped quatrefoils and shields epitomised the spirit of the fifteenth century and appeared on the sides. Then, and in the following century, the chest was surmounted by a thick stone slab which was either chamfered or moulded at the edges. The base of the chest rested on a simple plinth. Prosperous people could afford fine tombs. The great 'wool' churches of East Anglia in particular and the Cotswolds to a lesser degree attest the generosity of the wealthy in the service of their God and in the expectation of prayers for their own souls. In these areas many chest tombs are extremely fine, in keeping with the benefactions within the church of the person they commemorate. Even so, the era of the ornate chest tomb was relatively short. Locally, the designers were often families of masons who worked within a fairly small area. They owe not only their prosperity to the cloth trade but the fact that they are remembered at all. Elsewhere good chest tombs in an otherwise indifferent churchyard usually indicate the last resting place of well-to-do families: gentry, farmers, landowners, millers and so on. Older, plainer chest tombs may be well scattered throughout that part of the churchyard which was in use when they were erected, but later ones tend to form family groups.

The chest tomb began to appear fairly frequently early in the seventeenth century. It was popular, if restrained in execution, throughout the century and reached its zenith with the Georgians. Early ones are most likely to be near the south door of the church. An odd but nonetheless similar monument is the carved slate slab on a brick base in the churchyard at **St Enodoc**, Cornwall. It is dated 1687 and is remarkable for the rustic incised figurework. The heavy ledger slab of a narrow seventeenth century chest tomb may well have served as a dole stone for the distribution of bread to the poor of the parish or some other charity. The proportions of the basic rectangle standardised during the seventeenth century to an equal width and height, and a length equal to the sum of both – the common 'double cube'. Plain panelling was sometimes done on all vertical surfaces, and in the eighteenth century these were often curved. The monument had a base and often a plinth, and the hitherto flat ledger might be capped with either a curved lid or one which was casket-shaped. Some of these were heavy in both design and execution, pyramidal or obelisk-shaped, and were topped by a finial. There are a number of these, in effect large caskets, around the Cotswolds. Elsewhere, a variation on the casket lid was the double gable arrangement.

The early eighteenth century chest tomb still had a heavy ledger slab, cut away on the underside to meet the top of the tomb below. There were table tombs, which, as the name suggests, comprised a flat slab with or without inscription or ornamentation on its surface, supported by a pillar at each corner resting on a flat base. The edges of both slab and base might be moulded or chamfered, the pillars plain or fluted. From the mid seventeenth century until well into the eighteenth a popular flamboyant Cotswold variation on the basic shape – mainly by way of decoration – was the lyre-shaped design to the ends. In this the upper edge of the tomb was continued outwards on each side as shoulders forming acanthus leaves which then curved inwards as they plunged downwards, ending in a loose coil which resembled the volute of an Ionic capital, although a rather more elongated one. The spaces between were filled with classical motifs: fruit and flowers, heads and symbols of death, eternity and triumph. With the Georgians came the fashion for Baroque-style chest tombs with turned balusters at the angles. Good examples of the seventeenth and eighteenth centuries are at **Chaddleworth**, Berkshire, **Painswick, Stroud, Daglingworth, Winson, Harescombe, Broadwell** and **Duntisbourne Rouse** in Gloucestershire, **Herstmonceux**, East Sussex, **Chard**, Somerset, and **Christleton**, Cheshire. In country areas which were not particularly wealthy, the chest tomb of the late eighteenth century is likely to be conservatively decorated in relief with an urn at the centre flanked by swags, fruit and flowers and corner drapes. Inscriptions are most usually on the sides, sometimes carved in oval plaques with decorated frames, and where there are two such inscriptions on either side of the chest they commemorate different members of the same family. Even the simplest chests commonly had their corners worked into pilasters or balusters.

Some of these monuments are protected by an iron grille or a set of taller railings. During the eighteenth century much very good ironwork was put up in the village churchyard by the local blacksmith. In Victorian times it became something of an art and whilst the height of tomb railings was reduced there was a great variety of shapes and appendages. Fleur-de-lis, vine-scroll and strawberry-leaf designs were popular. There are fine examples at **St Illtyd**, Gwent, and **Madeley**, Shropshire. Work on the five exposed surfaces of the chest was still restrained, but now the corners might be inset by square colonettes with caps and bases. Classical motifs continued to predominate, heavily mixed with symbolism. The sides were invariably treated as panels with figurework, usually symbolic of death and the Resurrection, symmetrically done on each side flanking a panel. Heavier decoration and figurework, perhaps the likeness of the deceased or the tools of his trade or calling, appeared on the ends of tombs. Pedestal tombs with urns as finials developed in the nineteenth century into the obelisk shapes on high bases.

Late nineteenth century families revived the popularity of the chest tomb, after something of a lull. Tombs of close relations may often be found grouped together in the churchyard. Most of these monuments record little more than the basic essentials and are not outstanding, and nineteenth century churchyard monuments in general were heavy and often depressing. Gothic revival tombs were overpowering, and otherwise there were many three-dimensional representations of the classical motifs with central urn design or something similar. The ledger of the chest might be used as the base for this kind of sculpture and, in such instances, the whole is sometimes surmounted by a canopy on corner pillars.

Bale tombs

Bale tombs are a predominantly east Cotswold variation on the basic chest tomb. The name is derived from the design and appearance of the semi-cylindrical stone which runs the length of the ledger slab on the top of the tomb below, in much the same way as one may find an effigy within the church. Such stones are deeply carved at regular intervals along their length with grooves which may run from the base of one side straight over the curving surface to the base of the other. On some the grooves run diagonally. It is widely assumed that they represent corded bales of cloth and that the tomb is therefore of a person connected with the wool trade, but this is not always the case. It has also been suggested that they may represent the corpse wrapped in a shroud of wool, the legal requirement when the industry was suffering hard times. The ends of the 'bale' usually took the form of a skull set in a scallop or shell, and the positioning of this symbol of death may give the real clue to exactly what the 'bale' represents. The decoration on the tomb below was as for other chest tombs of the period. Bale tombs can be seen in many Gloucestershire and Oxfordshire churchyards; there are particularly good examples at

Stow-on-the-Wold, Asthall, Swinbrook, Fairford, Bibury, Burford and **Letcombe Regis**.

Tea-caddy tombs

Another Cotswold variation on the chest tomb, dating from the eighteenth century, is the tea-caddy tomb, although eccentric tombs elsewhere may resemble it in basic shape even if made at a different period. The tea-caddy is tall in relation to its ground area, as if the chest has been set at ninety degrees to its normal position. It may be rectangular, circular or square in plan and sometimes tapered or topped by a lid with some kind of finial. The latter could be a ball, an urn or some similar device. The amazing churchyard at **Painswick**, Gloucestershire, has several amongst its treasures. Others may be found at – for example – **Withington**, Gloucestershire, and **Kington St Michael**, Wiltshire.

6. Detached towers

The largest building in the churchyard, other than the church itself, may be a detached or freestanding tower, belfry or campanile. No bell tower is in a more romantic position than the small thirteenth century structure, with its slate pyramidal cap, built into a rock right on the sea edge at **Gunwalloe**, Cornwall. A low tower, of the same date but with a gabled roof, is also built into a rock at **Lamorran** in the same county. **Henllan**, Clwyd, is also built on a rock. At **Combe**, Berkshire, is a freestanding bell turret which seems to be a kind of hybrid: a two-stage structure with all-round lean-to roofs forming aisles around the interior arrangement of beamwork, and a square stage above with a pyramidal cap. The whole is faced with shingles.

In marshlands, where the ground was not compact or solid, the distribution over so small a ground area of the great weight of a complete tower might cause settlement, structural problems or even collapse. In putting towers away from the church where there might be problems of this type, the builders were at least ensuring that any shift would not endanger the main fabric of the building. It is probable that a number of western towers, irrespective of the area in which they were built, were neither originally planned as the integral part of the church they are now, nor were they so erected. Although detached, they were built on the same plane as the naves, which were later extended to meet them. This occurred at **Terrington St John**, Norfolk. Elsewhere one may discern awkward joints in the masonry where towers which now open on to the nave were once buttressed on their east face – a sign that they were formerly detached.

Although builders feared that collapse might damage the rest of the church, some quite substantial detached towers were put up only a few feet from it. Others were erected as much as 70 feet (21 m) away, as in the case of **West Walton,** Norfolk. Almost a medieval gatehouse in its position, this thirteenth century building stands above open arches near the entrance to the churchyard. It is in three imposing stages, with octagonal corner buttresses to its full height, and has pointed blind arcades, niches and lights in the stages. At nearby **Terrington St Clement** the tower just meets with the church at its north-west angle but may be considered as detached since it was so built. Also in Norfolk is the detached round tower at **Little Snoring,** the Norman survivor of a church which is no longer there, and a four-stage structure was put up at **East Dereham,** Norfolk, in the sixteenth century.

Tydd St Giles, Cambridgeshire, is another church which seems to have all but banished its tower, a thirteenth century building with an upper storey of fifteenth century brick, standing some 50 feet (15 m) to the south of the main building. At **East Bergholt,** Suffolk, there is a very rustic-looking single-storey bell house beside a church which has an uncompleted tower. The bell house has a grille of wooden banding above vertical timber boarding on its sides, and the whole is topped by a steep, pyramidal roof with a louvred top. There are two detached towers in Suffolk: at **Bramfield** the circular tower is to the south-west of the church and at **Beccles** there is a huge Perpendicular structure with battlements and niches, lying to the south-east of the church.

The steeple at **Fleet,** Lincolnshire, has a three-stage tower with a stair turret, embattled parapet, stepped and gabled buttresses. Above is the spire, connected by flying buttresses. It was built in the fourteenth century to the south-west of the church. At **Long Sutton** in the same county a lead spire rises above the thirteenth century three-stage detached tower with its lancet windows and octagonal turrets at the belfry stage. The tower arches below were once open. There is a detached wooden turret at **Wix,** Essex. The fifteenth century tower at **Standon,** Hertfordshire, was built away from the church to the south-east and was later connected to the chancel by an organ chamber. In Bedfordshire there is a massive, vaulted detached tower at **Marston Moretaine,** built diagonally to the church in the fourteenth century. In the fifteenth century the four-stage battlemented tower was put up at **Elstow,** Bedfordshire. There, a stair turret rises above, there are two two-light bell openings on each face of the belfry stage and the whole is surmounted by a sharp spike.

The detached tower at **Ledbury,** Herefordshire, has a spire and other examples in the same county are the fourteenth century tower at **Richards Castle,** which has a pyramidal roof, a thirteenth century tower with lancets at **Bosbury** and another of the same date at **Garway.** The last is big and unbuttressed with a pyramidal roof and was connected to the nave by a covered passageway in the seventeenth century. There is a timber-framed belfry on the detached tower at **Holmer** and a timber bell stage on the belfry at **Yarpole**. Perhaps the best known of the detached buildings in Herefordshire churchyards is the belfry at **Pembridge**. A mass of wooden beamwork inside, this fourteenth century construction rises in three stages from an octagonal base of masonry, through two square timber stages, and ends in a narrow, pyramidal cap. In Gloucestershire there is a detached thirteenth century tower with spire at **Westbury-on-Severn** and at **Berkeley** the tower was put up in 1753 on medieval foundations. The tower at **Lapworth**, Warwickshire, was built in the fourteenth century, attached to the north-east angle of the nave.

The two remaining detached buildings in Wales are the fourteenth century belfry with its pyramidal cap at **Bronllys**, Powys, and the tower which was once part of an earlier church but now stands alone at **Llangyfelach**, West Glamorgan. Apart from those already mentioned, Cornwall has a tower which was built on to thirteenth century masonry to the south of the church at **Talland**, one of the thirteenth century with a pyramidal cap of slate at **Feock**, and another similar at **Gwennap**; a belfry at **Mylor** is made of wood and has a gabled roof, and a fifteenth century tower at **Illogan** has lost its church. At **Brookland**, Kent, there is a magnificent wooden structure which was built in the mid thirteenth century; there is nothing else like it and it stands close by a church of great interest to the visitor. There is a campanile on an adjacent hill at **Kirkoswald**, Cumbria. At **Chiseldon**, Wiltshire, the porch/tower, although not truly detached, has the south clerestory running behind it and is virtually a detached tower.

7. On the church

Wall markings

Few external consecration crosses exist, having been either eroded away by the elements or covered by subsequent wall resurfacing. In the early days of Christianity it was the altar alone which was consecrated, and at all times the altars of a church were afforded special consideration in the service. Yet long before the Conquest the service encompassed the whole church. Throughout the middle ages the bishop marked twelve crosses with oil on both the inside and outside of the building, one for each article in the Creed. Internally these were painted, but those on outside walls were later incised or affixed in metal. Otherwise the outline might be picked out in stone, for example hard flint in a freestone wall. Every church is dedicated to God. The service of consecration, before allowing in the laity, gave it the name of a saint into whose care were henceforth entrusted the souls of those who worshipped there.

Masons' marks appear on individual features within the church and on internal and exterior walls which have not been scraped or rendered and are of ashlar. The idea of a mason or master mason putting his own mark on his work is thought to date from the Romans, and the practice became common in Britain after the Conquest. The mason had an individual mark which he put on his dressed stone before it was used. These marks tended to be basic geometrical shapes, stylised initials, lines and angles with an additional stroke or figure to make them individual. Some had the definite outline of birds or animals, often those of symbolic or religious significance. This trade mark or signature was often passed on to a mason's descendant in the same trade, who simply added a further figure – another branch to the same pedigree. Many of them became quite complicated designs. The mark identified a mason's personal work and his output. Today we can use them to check on the standard of workmanship and the area over which a particular mason or his descendants worked. They may also be a useful guide to the length of time taken to build a church which is all of the same period.

Masons' marks should not be confused with votive or pilgrims' crosses. These were scratched or incised, often around the entrance, by travellers or others as evidence of a vow, or by knights or crusaders. They are usually small and can be easily overlooked.

Sundials

Some form of sundial has been used, associated with the church and primarily to indicate the times for its services, from the days when the Anglo-Saxons incised scratch or mass dials on stone slabs attached to the south-facing exteriors of their churches. Dials may be static or portable. Whilst most of the examples extant remain, if not *in situ*, then certainly in a similar position, there are some Saxon carvings which may then or later have done the office of a sundial but now are built elsewhere into the wall of the church. The Madonna and Child at **Inglesham**, Wiltshire, now low down on the interior south wall of the little chapel, is an example. At **Kirkdale**, North Yorkshire, the signed, late Saxon (*c* 1060) dial has a long explanatory inscription in heavy carving on slabs. Hands are sculpted around the dial at **North Stoke**, Oxfordshire, and that at **Bishopstone**, East Sussex, includes a cross. There is a Saxon mass dial at **Saintbury**, Gloucestershire.

The concept of the sundial originated in the ancient world, but its principle was easily and universally grasped. The sun daily traversed the sky – although people did not know how or why – in what appeared to be a regular fashion. The shadow cast by a stationary object moved around at the same speed each day as the relative position of the sun changed. Hence the shadow from an intervening metal pin or rod, called a *gnomon*, fixed into the church wall, would fall along the same plane each day at the same time. The particular interest was in noon and the times of the important church services, mass and vespers (evensong). These were sometimes indicated by incised lines which radiated from the central pin, that of mass at nine o'clock in the morning being more strongly cut than others.

Anglo-Saxon dials gave only a rough approximation of the time between sunrise and sunset. Some were quartered into three-hour 'tides' which equated with the length of the old Roman watches. This meant that whilst, in practice, the quarters each side of midday remained constant, the length of the other two depended upon the season of the year. Others divided daytime into anything up to twelve sections on the vertical face of the slab. Sunrise and sunset were indicated as halves of the same horizontal base line, and midday by a vertical incision at right angles which joined the base line midway along its length. The figure was usually bisected by intermediate lines at forty-five degrees. An example of the twelfth century, which includes cable moulding, is at **Marsh Baldon**, Oxfordshire.

The sundial seems generally not to have been developed either architecturally or as a decorative feature between the twelfth and fifteenth centuries. Some materials, particularly slate, took the better and more lasting work. Most wall dials extant are of this period, and they are numerous and for the most part uninteresting. They comprise simple scratch dials as at **Westham**, East Sussex, carved straight into the exterior stonework of the church with indifferent spacing between the radiating lines, which also varied in number. At **Baydon**, Wiltshire, there is one on its side and another inverted.

Old dials can be found almost anywhere on the south-facing walls of churches, but many are not obvious. A favourite position was above the doorway of the south porch; others were on buttresses and at the south-west corner of the building. In Cornwall there are many fine examples cut into slate. They may include the name of the maker, be dated and have witty thoughts or amusing verses which mostly concern the passage of time. Their content echoes, perhaps mockingly, the sentiments expressed by way of puns and such like in the epitaph and tombstone descriptions to be found in the churchyard. Much of what is said about lettering forms on churchyard monuments (see 'Headstones' in chapter 5) applies to sundials. There is an ambitious dial set on little corbels at **Eyam**, Derbyshire, which tells world time, and that of 1757 at **Tawstock**, Devon, records the hour in various cities of the world.

While slate weathers well, outside the slate-producing regions most wall dials will have long since lost their gnomons and be themselves eroded. A large outward-splayed hole where the gnomon once was means that as this rusted it wore away the stonework until it dropped out. What are left may be faint rough circles with a central hole and lines radiating from it about fifteen degrees apart. It was in the fifteenth century that the day was first divided into twenty-four hours and mechanical clocks came into general use. Vertical sundials were then adapted more as general timepieces than specific reminders of services, with the number of each hour cut or marked at the end of each line.

There are a good many examples extant from the sixteenth, seventeenth and eighteenth centuries. The one great problem with sundials was that they could only be relied upon during daylight hours when it was sunny, and they were no use for indicating when the church bells should be rung for mass and vespers in winter. Mechanical clocks and watches were more reliable and the sundial became more of an ornamental feature in the churchyard than a necessity. The gnomon was placed above an horizontal surface on a freestanding pillar. At **Tilston**, Cheshire, the sundial is now where the head of the churchyard cross once was. Inigo Jones's design at **Chilham**, Kent, is an example of a beautiful pedestal dial which is more ornamental than of practical use. There is a heavy rectangular sundial just inside the churchyard at **Upton St Leonards**, Gloucestershire. At **Godshill**, Isle of Wight, the sundial is on a cross and at **Wymondham**, Leicestershire, it is on the stump of one. **Bootle**, Cumbria, has a very tall one, and at **Newbiggin** in the same county is a medieval dial on a buttress. **Christleton**, Cheshire, has one on a pillar. At **Ightham**, Kent, the sundial is dated 1669, and also from the seventeenth century is one on a wooden post at **Aldbury**, Hertfordshire. The dial with symbolic crossed bones at **Zennor**, Cornwall, is dated 1737, that at **Pilling**, Lancashire, was made in 1766 and the dial on the south porch at **Clare**, Suffolk, was put up in 1790. Another from the eighteenth century is at **St Just**, Cornwall. Early nineteenth century examples can be seen at **Tedburn St Mary**, Devon, and **Seaton Ross**, North Humberside.

8. Fauna and flora

All churchyards support some wildlife and the range is often surprisingly large. Some species like house sparrows or the swifts which swirl and dip around the tower during the day and the bats which do so at night make their homes on or in the church building. Bats, usually the pipistrelle, may be seen hanging from roof beams. An owl may flap away as one enters the churchyard and might even be seen inside the church. A skylark might have its nest amidst the churchyard grass. Botanists and naturalists may be encountered enthusiastically poking around where the ground is damp or slopes into a ditch which is partly filled by stagnant water. Artists, too, come to sketch or paint the wild flowers which grow in the grounds, knowing that they are likely to find plenty to choose from. Sometimes groups of them may be seen at work in large country churchyards like **Lavenham**, Suffolk.

It is not difficult to understand why the range is so good, or indeed why there may be species of plants growing in a churchyard which are not native to the area. Even in rural parts, the churchyard may be the last small patch of ground which man has not tried to cultivate in some way, apart perhaps from an annual haymaking of the long grass. There will have been no crop spraying, no systematic and seasonal churning up of the land. Any seeds dropped by passing birds or carried on the wind may there stand the best chance of establishing themselves in the area. Plants which are peculiar to a particular area may be seen in the churchyard, if nowhere else, and may there stand their best chance of survival. If this is true of the country churchyard, how much more noticeable and important are these factors in the precinct surrounding a town church. Left to their own devices and not cleared out by over-zealous gardeners, species of plants can develop over a period of time, introducing themselves into new areas and becoming established. In industrial towns the churchyard may well be the only place in which one may see a variety of birds and hear them sing.

Perhaps the most beautiful and the most primitive form of life in the churchyard is likely to be a type of lichen, adhering to stonework or trees. The colour varies depending on the area but may commonly be in shades of grey, green, yellow and red. Lichens are slow growing associations of fungus and alga which reproduce when spores drop from one growth, provided that the cells of both again come into contact with each other. The resulting crust grows by feeding entirely on the atmosphere, which is why it may eventually cover whole areas of apparently barren rock or stonework. Its method of feeding means that it is particularly sensitive to air pollution and will not grow where there is a high level of sulphur dioxide, such as in towns. But it does not need water to survive and is extremely long lived. Look for lichen on the walls of any old country church, on monuments and stonework in the churchyard and on stone walls surrounding it.

Walls are a haven for a great deal of wildlife. Mosses and fungi grow from them as they do from trees, and saxifrage may have taken root in the crevices along with pellitory of the wall, a perennial with green flowers. Look for frogs and toads at the base where it is likely to be both warm and damp, and do not, on a hot afternoon, be surprised to encounter a grass snake or adder basking in the warmth of a broken-down wall. A snake may also be seen on a grassy bank in the summer, where the churchyard may have been artificially built up to a higher level for extra burials in the twentieth century and then slopes sharply away.

More unusual birds are generally present in churchyards which include a range of conifers. The little goldcrest is particularly at home there, as are blue tits. Apart from nesting in the trees, they feed on the berries. Some, like the tree-creeper, nest inside loose bark whilst woodpeckers make their nests within the trunks. If the churchyard includes beech trees, one may see jays, which are particularly fond of beechnuts. Any tall trees, such as elms and oaks, will attract colonies of chattering rooks and crows, and elms — now sadly much depleted — are a great favourite with jackdaws, woodpeckers, kestrels and wood pigeons. Oak trees have a particular religious significance as the Celtic druids worshipped in their groves. The trees themselves provide food for many species of insects, which in turn feed a variety of birds such as the nuthatch and chaffinch. Amongst the roots and in the boles of the larger trees, as well as along the hedges, may be woodmice, shrews and bank voles, perhaps hedgehogs and rats. Whilst the smaller mammals forage for insects, grasses and other seeds they will be preyed upon by weasels on the ground, owls and kestrels from above. Amongst the smaller trees may be hazel, lime and ash. The ash has been associated with religion in Britain since ancient times. The invading Vikings, whose art appeared on early decorated stonework together with Anglo-Saxon Christian and pagan art, favoured the ash and dedicated it to their god Thor.

Evergreens have long played a significant part in religious ceremonies and it is not accidental that churchyards are frequently full of them. The red berries produced by several species have symbolic associations with the blood of Christ. Churchyard evergreens were used for strewing in the church at certain festivals as a substitute for palm leaves, which were not available to people in Britain. The act was symbolic of the Jewish custom of waving palm branches at their feasts, applied to the triumphal entry of Jesus into Jerusalem on the first day of the Week of Passion, but it may have meant no more than that waving around evergreens and decorating the church with them was a pleasant and pretty thing to do, especially at the village feast or at Christmas when the people were at their happiest.

But there are likely to have been other, pagan precedents. Apollo, emblem of the sun, was associated with the laurel as a symbol of immortality, which the god himself enjoyed through eternal youth. The evergreen was dedicated to his temple and his honour and hence was extensively used by his followers. Laurel bushes have been popular in the churchyard since their introduction to Britain in the sixteenth century. Most churchyards contain some ivy and very many seem to be almost held together by it.

Like holly, which also appears in churchyards, it may have had some significance in pagan times when both were used as decoration and ivy may well be the all-embracing vine depicted on early church art. Left to its own devices it quickly spreads over monuments and walls, entwines itself around trees and inextricably conjoins with brambles. Within and beneath it, however, will be insects and grubs in profusion and so it will attract the small animals and birds which prey upon them. Brambles too have their visitors; butterflies enjoy the soft fruit as do wasps and other insects, most of which are to the taste of blackbirds.

Hedges have long since ceased to be simply the barriers for which purpose the Saxons began to plant them. They are full of life, continually renewing themselves, and host to birds, mammals and insects. Hawthorn in particular, favoured for eighteenth century land enclosures, provides food and shelter for insects and berries for birds.

Gosforth, Cumbria, has a cork tree which was planted in 1833. There are elms at **Ross-on-Wye**, Herefordshire, and lots of rose bushes at **Boughton Monchelsea**, Kent. **St Newlyn East**, Cornwall, has a fig tree growing out of the churchyard wall and there is a spina Christi tree at **Herstmonceux**, East Sussex. The willow at **Ashburton**, Devon, is reputed to be descended from one at St Helena, and at **Colaton Raleigh**, Devon, a colony of bees has lived in a hole in the sandstone tower for as long as anyone can remember. **North Luffenham**, Leicestershire, has a walnut tree and, in the same county, there are limes at **Sharnford**. A cedar grows at **Norton**, Kent, and **Barham** has beeches. Often the pathway to the churchyard is lined with trees of the same kind, poplars, limes, laurels and beeches being favourites.

An east London churchyard is being developed as an educational nature reserve. The 9 acres (3.6 ha) of St Mary Magdalene churchyard, **East Ham**, is now the responsibility of the Passmore Edwards Museum, and an interpretative centre is being provided.

Yews

A seemingly essential feature of the churchyard, especially in southern England but also elsewhere in soil which is chalky or where there is limestone, is *Taxus baccata* – the evergreen native yew tree. In southern areas there was little choice for a native evergreen, the yew being almost the only species. It has a characteristically fluted trunk and gnarled branches, and its dense foliage may engulf large areas of the churchyard. But it can be clipped almost without limit and, as has been found necessary in the case of many aged examples which have grown dangerously out of shape, will withstand major tree surgery. Some smaller churchyard yews are kept in order by gentle topiary. But wherever they are found as trees, they set the scene of the churchyard; their height in the foreground or middle distance often balances that of the church and their characteristic smell pervades the grounds. They seem solid and peaceful, the close nature of the foliage providing cool cover on hot sunny days.

There are enormous or aged yew trees all over the south of England. Fine examples exist at **Selborne**, Hampshire, **Wilmington**, East Sussex, and **Crowhurst**, Surrey. Many are as much as eight hundred years old and church guidebooks often claim an astonishing age for their yews. Certainly some may be older than the nearby church. Pre-Christian use of the site may have included pagan ceremonies in which yew foliage played a part. Legend associates the frequency of churchyard yews with evergreens which supposedly gave shelter to the first Christian missionaries. Yet they were considered to be sacred before these missionaries made their mark, the evergreen foliage being symbolic of everlasting life. In *The Forest Trees of Britain,* published in 1903, the Reverend C. A. Johns conjectured: 'There is a far greater possibility that at the period when crosses were erected in these sacred spots as emblems of victory over death achieved by the Author of our faith, the yew tree was stationed not far off to symbolise, by its durability and slowly altering features, the patient waiting for the resurrection by those who committed the bodies of their friends to the ground in hope.'

A lot of yew trees were planted by the clergy after the Conquest. Edward I decreed that they should be planted to protect the church from the elements. This was usually done on the south side, one near to the main pathway and sometimes another on the way to a secondary entrance. Planting them opposite porches helped to protect the doorways. Medieval longbows and staves were said to have been made of yew wood, although it is doubtful whether much of it came from village churchyards. Large quantities were imported, and the only association the churchyard may have had with yew wood in weaponry was when the grounds were used for archery practice. The suggestion that arrows were made locally from this wood is now refuted, in contrast to the belief of only a few years ago. Yet the yew's incredibly slow rate of growth gives it an elasticity which makes it suitable for all the items mentioned. Villagers would have carried the foliage in Easter processions and spread it over graves. In some areas it was planted on new graves or placed beneath the corpse either on the ground or in the coffin. Yew foliage would never have been found inside the house as, indoors, it was considered to be a harbinger of death.

The oldest tombs and headstones will often be found under the dense umbrella of foliage of a great churchyard yew. They may have been put there when the tree was but a sapling. Sadly, although its compact foliage and low spreading habit protected such memorials from the elements, it also hid any secular and unauthorised activity around them. Tombs and headstones thus hidden are consequently often in a poor state of repair and disarray or may have graffiti on them. Sometimes this may be quite interesting; vandalism is by no means a twentieth century innovation. For the researcher into family history, a single churchyard yew might hide a large piece of genealogy.

This venerable growth has not always been seen at its best. In 1854 a *Rural Encyclopaedia* said: 'This tree has usually been seen by the present and last generations of Britons in a state of tortured growth or in an old, declining, or diseased condition ... it used to be planted in and near burying grounds in Britain in the same way as the cypress is in other countries, but ... it is now seldom employed in that way; and when the auracarias and the many recently introduced pendulous and fastigiate trees become better known, it will probably lose altogether its sepulchral association.' In its natural state the yew will repay a study of its bird life, for the berries are not poisonous to the birds as the foliage is to cattle. Indeed, the yew hedge was seen as a deterrent to cattle entering the churchyard.

There is a famous yew tree at **Edington**, Wiltshire. Most ancient ones which still exist have an element of folklore about them. At **Wroughton** in the same county it is said that a ghost may be raised by walking three times around the churchyard yew and pushing a pin into its trunk. The ninety-nine yews at **Painswick**, Gloucestershire, are world famous. They were planted at the end of the eighteenth century and legend insists that it is impossible to grow one hundred. They are kept neatly clipped. Elsewhere they are associated with sheltering ghosts at night. At **Broad Clyst**, Devon, there are yews all around the churchyard and at **Barford**, Warwickshire, they line the path to the porch. Those at **Preston**, Lancashire, are reputed to come from the Garden of Gethsemane. There is a ring of them around the church at **Llansantffraed-in-Elwell**, Powys, and some which form a tunnel at **Dunsfold**, Surrey. Other notable yews can be found at **Iffley**, Oxfordshire, **Helmdon**, Northamptonshire, **Ulcombe**, Kent, **Darley Dale**, Derbyshire, **Tangmere**, West Sussex, and **Stoke Gabriel**, Devon.

9. Building materials

The church is the most important building in the churchyard. Yet most people are less inclined to notice its exterior than view it from within, and unless they have specific business in the grounds or otherwise have their attention drawn to something of interest, they usually hurry inside. So far this book has been mostly concerned with the churchyard itself, but now we turn our attention to that part of the church which is viewed from the churchyard – the exterior. When pilgrims in the middle ages were almost safely home, or travellers who were weary of the road were in want of lodgings, it was the church in the distance which indicated they had not far to go. The sight of the church must have revived flagging spirits and put renewed urgency into heavy steps. Often visible for miles, especially if built on high ground – or indeed in a vale to which the approach was hilly – it was the object they might watch from when it was a dot on the horizon. Yet long before he saw his own church, the traveller might know he was nearing home by the shape and size of others, or by the types of local stone used in their construction, churchyard walls and even monuments. Throughout Britain there are local materials, styles of building and characteristics which epitomise the regions in which they are found. This applies to churchyard walling and the style and types of churchyard monuments as it does to the church itself.

The character and colouring of churchyard walls and memorials, as well as of the church itself, and often its size, were determined by three main factors. These were the availability of materials, the types used, and the degree of expertise by then acquired by the masons and builders. A number of other factors affected what was done with stone in the hands of the workers. These included the wealth of the area, religious influences, architectural and artistic influence from both home and abroad and the physical properties of the stone itself. The type of stone also accounts for the extent of any subsequent deterioration, for some types weather less well than others. Inland quarries provided stone locally as well as to parts of adjacent counties. The cost of carrying stone overland in the middle ages was high, and it was more easily done by water. Even so, there were very many small local quarries, long since disused. It is there that one is most likely to find the type of stone used in nearby medieval churches, walls and monuments. Foreign building materials as well as those from English coastal quarries were used elsewhere on the coast and in inland areas which could be reached by rivers. The countryside was first opened up in this respect by the canal system of the eighteenth century, but it was the railways of the nineteenth century which put building stone from favoured quarries within the reach of architects and builders everywhere.

The earliest constructional material for churches in England was wood because it was naturally plentiful and accessible to all. It was also used for coffins from the earliest times as well as pre-Conquest churchyard memorials. Large amounts of timber continued to go into the making of many country churches until the fourteenth century and it was always popular in the stoneless areas. Less stable than stone, it is liable to warp with the elements even when used as covered framework. It is also perishable. Even so, its composition enabled it to be easily and exquisitely carved, making it so suitable for furnishings and interior work that the crafts of carpenter, joiner and woodcarver were to become the most skilful and widely represented in the churches of England. In the churchyard, timber was used structurally as beams, struts and braces in lychgates and belfries, and in gates and fencing.

Wood continued to be used for roofing, framework, spires, porches, belfry stages and towers, particularly of the half-timbered kind. Many belfry stages were built on low brick or stone tower bases; otherwise some fine wooden detached belfries were constructed (see chapter 6).

The best general material used for church building in England was oolitic limestone: freestone of the Jurassic limestone belt which curves from Chesil Bank to the Humber, embracing seven counties, but also enabling good building and carving to be done in adjacent areas. Limestone is composed of grains of calcium carbonate and yields blocks of different sizes which can be easily dressed and weather well. Such blocks were used in the making of churches and churchyard walls. The more compact types take such a high polish that they are locally termed 'marbles' and have from time to time been much in demand for interior furnishings, decorative and structural work.

Limestone is particularly rich in animal and vegetable fossil remains, and the shelly type from Purbeck was, when polished, highly favoured by architects in the middle ages. True marble is white and composed of very fine grains of calcite. When polished it acquires a waxy surface and is used for monuments.

The purest form of limestone is chalk, softer in the southern counties than in the north, where it hardens into limestone. This white substance is not generally thought of as a constructional material although many downland churches have pillars or arcades which are made of it. Most of these buildings are small and unpretentious. Chalk is also found between the stone ribs of vaulting, as internal dressings, and sometimes as facing for internal walls.

Associated with chalk is flint, small pieces of lustrous crystalline silica which can be picked from the surface of the ground. Its potential seems largely to have been disregarded abroad, but in England flint adorns both small country churches and large wool churches to great effect. It is predominant as a building material in the stoneless eastern counties and the downland areas of south-eastern and central southern England. Flint may be coloured black, dark brown, grey or yellowish brown. Whilst it is brittle and easy to break, it is very hard wearing and cannot be carved. It is mainly used for walling either by itself or in conjunction with brick or with pieces of freestone, where small quantities of stone were available. Flint may be encountered laid at random or in courses.

This is not to be confused with the decorative treatment of flint as the fine flushwork of East Anglia. There, a framework of thin stone strips was filled with blue-black knapped or square chipped pieces of flint. This formed an exquisite chequerboard patterning which sometimes contained freestone tracery or motifs such as initials or symbols. The arrangement might decorate the whole wall surface of the church or be confined to porches, parapets, buttresses, clerestories or the lower parts of towers. Gateposts were sometimes similarly treated.

Limestone and sandstone both provided ashlar, to be used as a surface to walls and in walling. As a surface dressing to the church proper, the infilling would have constituted a coarser material. While some areas had little option but to build with rough stone, ashlar was a considerable improvement. Elsewhere it marked a medieval decline in practical masonry. Much later it was revived to hide red brick as this went out of fashion. Ashlar is properly the name given to blocks of stone as they arrive from the quarries for the purpose of surfacing the walls, squared but not finished. Whether it then becomes plain, tooled, random tooled, rustic or broken depends on the subsequent surface treatment it receives and the tools with which this is done. Blocks were not usually thick but of standard sizes which varied over the centuries, generally becoming larger in surface area. They were carefully and uniformly squared so that they could be skilfully laid in level, horizontal courses with the minimum of mortar between. Ashlar was finished on its external face – in the case of softer stone – by abrading with sand and water to remove any tooling and provide a plain surface. Otherwise it was sawn and hewn with axe, bolster or chisel. The masons of each period used their tools in ways which were peculiar to them, leaving distinctive markings on their work.

In many areas the churches and churchyard walls are built entirely of sandstone, particularly in the west, midlands and northeast. This material is composed of compacted grains of sand together with some cementing agent, producing textures which may be fine or coarse-grained and an almost infinite variety of colours. Sandstones with large, coarse grains are called gritstones. Although those of the older formations produce the best building stone of its kind, it is generally an inferior material which is porous and weathers poorly. Sandstone churches are more likely to have been patched up or later added to in brick. In industrial areas they may have seriously discoloured, often turning quite black.

Granite is the hard stone found chiefly in the far west and north-west. It consists of quartz, felspar and mica, a mixture of crystals which are opaque, grey and flesh-coloured. The ratio of the mix gives granite either a silver, brown, grey, grey-green or pink appearance. The amount of quartz determines the hardness of the stone, and the felspar is the component most likely to decay. Granite churches are of sombre and austere appearance. For, whilst granite takes a high polish, it is difficult to carve and undercut, so it does not admit decoration in high relief. It may be very grainy but in good quality granite the grains are evenly distributed. Large pieces which could be picked up in Cornwall and used for walling were known as 'moorstone', but it was not extensively quarried until the great wave of church building in the fifteenth century. Very large blocks of granite can be obtained.

Both the Anglo-Saxons and the Normans found new uses for Roman bricks, although builders did not learn how to construct with them properly until Tudor times. Brick buildings were popular in the sixteenth and seventeenth centuries; brick was a boon to the stoneless areas both as a substitute for rubble walling and later as surface material. It accounts for a variety of colours, mostly reds and blues caused by variations in the clay beds. Whilst bricks have always been of uniform sizes, they were hand-made until the middle of the nineteenth century. Brick churches were built in Tudor times, during the Victorian and Edwardian periods and to a lesser extent into the twentieth century, generally of deep pink brick. Old stone churches were rebuilt in brick or added to by perhaps constructing a chancel or arcade in the material. The Tudors introduced patterns and courses into their brickwork, using two main methods. The length of a brick is called the *stretcher;* the *header* is its depth. 'English' bond is a method of laying stretchers and headers in alternate courses and 'Flemish' bond has alternate stretchers and headers in the same course.

Following the Conquest cargoes of creamy yellow oolitic limestone were shipped to England from Caen on the river Orne in Normandy, close to the English Channel. Although native English stone was used where possible for building churches, large quantities of Caen stone were imported during the twelfth and thirteenth centuries for use in constructing cathedrals, abbeys, castles and churches. Large consignments were ordered for stoneless areas where there was much work to be done. In eastern and south-eastern counties it was used in conjunction with expensive native stone, which had to be sparingly apportioned, and usually reached its destination on barges drawn along natural waterways. Caen stone is soft when quarried and easy to work but hardens on exposure to the atmosphere. In England it is better suited for internal work, and it is effectively used for figurework and sculptured furnishing, tombs and canopies, reredoses, screens, fonts and pulpits. Otherwise it was used in non-stone areas for window tracery and frames, doorways and decorative features such as carved gargoyles and pinnacles.

Kentish ragstone was used in churches of the south-east, where good natural building stone was scarce, and in the churches of Victorian London. It is a hard, calcareous sandstone, brown or bluish grey, shelly and brittle, which gives a coarse uneven surface to walls. It cannot be dressed or used as quoins or dressings. It is obtained from coastal Lower Greensand deposits.

Alabaster is a semi-translucent sulphate of lime which is chiefly found in central and north-eastern England. It is soft and can be exquisitely carved and polishes to a pearly finish. A favourite for figurework and statuary between the fifteenth and seventeenth centuries, when most of it was probably imported from the continent, alabaster was revived by the Victorians, who loved polished marbles and used it to make fonts and pulpits. Pure white forms come from Italy, but those quarried in England are off-white with reddish brown veins and irregular markings. It is this which is most often encountered as effigies, monuments and tombs in country churches.

Churches are commonly roofed with thatch, wooden shingles, roofing tiles, stone, metal and slate. The best material is stone. The most beautiful roofs are those of brown, hand-made medieval tiles; the worst are the machine-made tiles of the Victorians. Roofing tiles were widely available by the beginning of the thirteenth century, but those of the fifteenth century were of such poor quality and indifferent sizing that standards were instituted towards the end of the century. They were made wherever suitable clay was available, although slate had long been used as a roofing material. A rash of solemn grey Welsh slate spread across England, relieved here and there by the grey or blue slate from the long established quarries of Cornwall and the blues and greens which came from the Lake District. Other slates were quarried in the west and north-east. Slate is not porous; it has an even colour and surface texture and is relatively cheap. It is perhaps the most practical roofing material.

10. Last word

There is no better way of discovering the churchyard than by doing something to record what is to be found there. The Council for British Archaeology (112 Kennington Road, London SE11 6RE) publishes a Newsletter and Calendar which lists rescue projects in churchyards amongst other schemes.

Even so, it is not what is buried that is in the most danger. The enduring nature of churchyard monuments, which most people take for granted, is anything but a fact. Those who feel that the contents of the grounds are of some value, for whatever reason, should be aware that others are embarking upon officially approved wholesale clearances without a thought for the historical and archaeological potential. The task of recording monuments and their inscriptions has become increasingly more important as churches are declared redundant or churchyards subjected to clearance and other approved schemes of a similar nature.

Such surveys are not difficult to do, but they demand time, patience and a systematic approach. Those interested in the practical aspects of recording the grounds should buy the CBA's inexpensive *How To Record Graveyards* by Jeremy Jones. It is a complete guide to the subject and all one needs to do a thoroughly professional job.

Bibliography

A companion volume, *Discovering Church Architecture* (1976), includes a comprehensive list of useful titles on this and related subjects. When *Discovering Churchyards* was first published (1982) it included a supplementary list of those titles which had come out in the years between. For this reprint the second list has been brought up to date, but it should still be read in conjunction with that in *Discovering Church Architecture*.

Addison, W. *Local Styles of the English Parish Church*. Batsford, 1982.

Anderson, W. *The Rise of Gothic*. Hutchinson, 1985.

Bailey, B. *Churchyards of England and Wales*. Hale, 1987.

Beaulah, K. *Church Tiles of the Nineteenth Century*. Shire, 1987.

Binney, M. *Save Churches at Risk*. Save Britain's Heritage, 1978.

Binney, M., and Burman, P. *Churches and Chapels — Who Cares?* BTA, 1977.

Blatch, M. *A Guide to London's Churches*. Constable, 1978.

Bond, F. *Fonts and Font Covers*. Waterstone, 1985.

Bowyer, J. *The Evolution of Church Building*. Crosby Lockwood, 1977.

Brabbs, D. *English Country Churches*. Weidenfeld and Nicolson, 1985.

Burgess, F. *English Churchyard Memorials*. Lutterworth Press, 1963.

Butler, L. A. S., and Morris, R. K. *The Anglo-Saxon Church*. CBA, 1986.

Cautley, H. M. *Suffolk Churches and Their Treasures*. Boydell and Brewer, 1982.

Cautley, H. M. *Norfolk Churches*. Boydell and Brewer, 1980.

Chatfield, M. *Churches the Victorians Forgot*. Moorland Publishing, 1979.

Child, M. *Discovering Church Architecture*. Shire, 1976.

Child, M. *English Church Architecture: A Visual Guide*. Batsford, 1981.

Cobb, G. *London City Churches*. Batsford, 1977.

Cocke, T. *Recording a Church: An Illustrated Glossary*. CBA, 1982.

Corke, J. (editor). *Suffolk Churches*. Suffolk HTC, 1976.

Council for Care of Churches. *Churchyard Handbook*. Church Information Office, 1976.

Crewe, S. *Visionary Spires*. Waterstone, 1986.

Cruden, S. *Scottish Medieval Churches*. Donald, 1986.

Dirsztay, P. *Church Furnishings*. Routledge and Kegan Paul, 1978.

Department of Environment. *New Life for Old Churches*. HMSO, 1977.

Elleray, D. R. *The Victorian Churches of Sussex*. Phillimore, 1980.

Greenoak, F. *God's Acre*. Orbis, 1985.

Hanna, M. *English Churches and Visitors*. English Tourist Board, 1984.

Hardy, P. *A Guide to the Care and Preservation of Medieval Cathedrals and Churches*. Construction Press, 1983.

Hayman, R. *Church Misericords and Bench Ends*. Shire, 1989.

Hibbert, C. *London's Churches*. Macdonald/Queen Anne Press, 1988.

Howell, P., and Sutton, I. *Faber Guide to Victorian Churches*. Faber, 1988.

Hough, J. *Essex Churches*. Boydell and Brewer, 1983.

Hudson, K. *Churchyards and Cemeteries*. Bodley Head, 1984.

Kemp, B. *Church Monuments*. Shire, 1985.

Kemp, B. *English Church Monuments*. Batsford, 1981.

Lindley, K. *Of Graves and Epitaphs*. Hutchinson, 1965.

Mansfield, H. O. *Norfolk Churches*. Terence Dalton, 1976.

Morshead, Sir O. *Dorset Churches*. Dorset HCT, 1975.

Platt, C. *Parish Churches of Medieval England*. Secker and Warburg, 1981.

Ponting, K. G. *Churches of Wessex*. Moonraker Press, 1977.

Randall, G. *The English Parish Church*. Batsford, 1982.

Riches, A. *Victorian Church Building and Restoration in Suffolk*. Boydell and Brewer, 1982.

Sinden, D. *The English Country Church*. Sidgwick and Jackson, 1988.

Starr, C. (editor). *A Guide to Essex Churches*. Essex CST, 1980.

Syms, J. A. *Kent County Churches*. Meresborough, 1984.

Verey, D. *Cotswold Churches*. Batsford, 1976.

Verey, D. (editor). *Gloucestershire Churches*. Alan Sutton, 1981.

Young, E. *London's Churches*. Grafton, 1986.

Index

INDEX